PRODIGY PERFORMANCE
HABITS

Rustin Matthew
Prodigy Performance Habits

All rights reserved
Copyright © 2024 by Rustin Matthew

Published by BooxAI
ISBN: 978-965-578-874-7

PRODIGY PERFORMANCE HABITS

RUSTIN MATTHEW

CONTENTS

DEDICATION

This book is dedicated to the loves of my life Tracy, Roxy and Hartley.

... and to Katie, who said that's the only thing that could get her to read a book!

... and to you, it's the audience that makes it special!

INTRODUCTION

HAVE MORE. DO MORE. BE MORE!

IT IS WHAT IT IS...

In an ever-evolving and fast-changing world, one thing is clear: the rules of the game are shifting, and we're advancing and progressing every day. Many of the old norms and industry conventions are rapidly becoming obsolete. It's now up to someone to determine the new rules, shape the path of our industry, and understand how dance training and performance fit into this era of groundbreaking technology. Who will lead the way and define the future of live entertainment? The answer is simple: Prodigy Performers, and that means you!

There have been countless times when I thought, "Why didn't they teach me that in school?" or "If I had known that at a younger age..." My goal with this book is to open your eyes to the habits that will empower you to adapt, rewrite, and personalize these rules, not just within the dance industry but in every aspect of life. By implementing the insights you gain from this book, you'll establish a solid foundation and cultivate the confidence to propel yourself forward. These habits will not only shape your future but also define your life and career. By embracing Prodigy Performance habits, you will have the power to create your own destiny.

You've grown up in an information age with social media and reality TV that has transformed everything. Today's dancers have access to information faster and more conveniently than ever before. Performers can instantly share their content and receive immediate feedback. This has changed the game on every level! Dance studios must now adapt to ever-changing trends more rapidly and push the envelope in regards to their dancers doing more earlier than ever. Because of this, training has become more efficient, and young dance athletes are achieving incredible feats at an earlier age. The best teachers and choreographers are just a click away, 24/7. The ability to brand yourself, market your talents, and create limitless content is at your fingertips.

So, the question becomes, how will you harness this unlimited potential? This is an incredible opportunity, but as the Peter Parker principle reminds us, "With great power comes great responsibility." What image do you want to portray to the world? What values do you stand for? When is the right time to act? There are so many questions, but don't worry; there are answers, too.

While some may argue about how to address these questions, I say, let's look at ourselves first, develop great personal habits, and decide who we want to be. Then, let's embrace the digital age and the opportunities it offers. The internet is here to stay, and our phones are integral to our lives.

The world will continue to evolve, with or without us. This means it's our responsibility to equip ourselves and the next generation of dancers with the best habits to navigate this changing landscape and create success in all areas. We achieve this by implementing Prodigy Performance habits, both mentally and physically. If you've been waiting to get started on a path of doing more and being more, your wait is over; it's "Go Time." If you're just beginning, if life has knocked you down, it's time to get back up, "Let's Go." If you're already doing well, and are living all your dreams, let's keep that ball rolling, you can achieve even greater heights. Regardless of where you are personally, the habits outlined in this book will propel you in the right direction and help you stay there. The journey continues. Take a deep breath and smile; this is just the beginning. I'm excited about your journey and the impact you'll make on the world.

IS THERE ANYTHING I CAN WORK ON?

"Is there anything I can work on?" This is a question I've been asked repeatedly after convention dance classes, rehearsals, and auditions, and it serves as one of the main catalysts for writing this book. In the early stages of my teaching career, I saw nothing wrong with this question and even encouraged it. I was delighted to be asked for my opinion, and I wanted dancers to take an active role in their learning. However, as I gained more experience and shifted my focus from myself to the students, I began to think, "Wow, if these dancers are truly looking for an edge, they could ask much more insightful questions." Many student truly fail to fully utilize all the great teachers they have access to.

While I continued to answer honestly and tried to provide as much guidance as I could, I found the question becoming somewhat cliché. I now recognize it as a potentially lazy and uninspiring inquiry. Of course, the short answer is always "yes," as there are always areas to improve. But I now expect more specificity. As a teacher who values both style and technique, I could easily provide a generic list of answers, a canned response, in the limited time available before or after a class or event. To be honest, many times, I also question how sincere this question even is! I often suspecting it might be something young dancers are told to ask by their parents or teachers, and they, in turn, ask it of every instructor. The reply goes in one ear and out the other as the main goal was to just ask a question, have some face time, and satisfy mom or their teacher. Let's flip that script!

In some sense, just asking that question is better than nothing, as it at least encourages interaction with instructors. But what if we aimed higher? What if we taught young dancers to ask more thoughtful questions and fostered strong Prodigy Performance habits from a young age? What if every dancer had a plan? What if dancers were aware of what they were working on and could pose precise questions instead of generic ones? What if they were accustomed to processing and applying information in every dance class and felt at ease with critical thinking? With these skills, they could ask more specific questions and use the answers to address their current concerns and areas of focus. This would allow more time and energy for everything. Allowing them to Have more, Do more, & Be more.

Undoubtedly, this approach would be far more efficient. It would also lead to better concentration and accelerated progress, thus helping you tackle your personal "to-do" list more effectively. If you're still genuinely asking, "Is there anything I can work on?" it's time to shift your focus to asking the right questions of the right people and becoming more detail-oriented in every aspect of your dance journey.

BUSY IS A CHOICE

Everything starts and ends with you, so let's clarify a few things. To begin, if you were content with mediocrity, you wouldn't have picked up this book in the first place. If it was given to you, consider it a gesture of love and belief in your potential. Give your benefactor a hug. They already see you as a Prodigy, or they believe you're on your way. It's time to give yourself the same credit. Often, things come to us precisely when we need them. I'm imagining that made you smile. Energies tend to attract similar energies. You might be reading this at a young age, free from entrenched habits that need correction. That's my greatest hope, you are about to save so much time! On the flip side, you could be stepping into or continuing on with a current dance career and this boost will refocus and motivate. Either way, the timing is perfect, and this book is exactly what you need. Embrace it. Learn, remember, and challenge ideas that clash with your current thoughts and beliefs. I know you're smiling because you know it's true. Keep reading; there's more.

No matter how much you've achieved so far, you're probably seeking more, something beyond what "normal" people settle for. You can't fathom a life of mundane mediocrity. Settling for replicating what others around you do is not an option, am I right? If you resonate with these sentiments, we're on the right track. But how do you get there? Your habits are how.

This book will spotlight a proven set of behaviors I hope you will soon call habits used by myself and other truly extraordinary dancers, choreographers, and industry professionals, whom I call Prodigy Performers or Prodigies for short. These exceptional individuals continually transcend what's considered achievable and normal in the dance world and beyond. Regardless of your age or current level, these habits work. When I mention "Prodigy Performer," I'm not only referring to performing on a stage. I mean performing in the broader context of how you approach each day on the stage of life - what you do and how you do it. Developing these exceptional habits will elevate your performance in all aspects of life. It's not arbitrary; it's a crafted and cultivated process that's available to you if you're willing to work on it. The secret is that it's as easy as you make it. Let's get to work.

• If you're a studio dancer in the world of competition and conventions aiming for a professional dance career, these habits are for you.

• If you already consider yourself a Prodigy and want to maintain that path while avoiding extended plateaus, these habits will bring clarity and continued success.

• If you have two left feet and don't have any dance-related aspirations but want to excel in various life endeavors, congratulations - you can also apply these habits to your goals.

This book may be directed at dancers, but it's ultimately about life. The bottom line is this: **Prodigy Performance habits work.**

Let's get straight to the point: Success doesn't happen to you; it happens because of you. Your thoughts and actions have brought you to where you are in your classes, your career, and your life. Now, it's time to align your habits with your thoughts and goals. This will propel you toward your dreams. Whether you're ten years old, striving to develop great habits from the start, or fifty years young, seeking to break and change unproductive habits that no longer serve you, it's vital to recognize your unused gifts and untapped potential. It's time to implement Prodigy Performance habits to propel you to the top and keep you there.

Throughout my years in dance studios, conventions, competitions, and the professional dance world, I've been repeatedly asked, "How is it done? How do you make it in the dance industry?" I've not only been asked how I've achieved success but also the million dollar question, "How others can replicate it in the current industry." What can parents do to ensure their child can have a professional performing career? Is there a secret recipe? What can I (or my dancer) do to "make it" in the dance industry? Unfortunately, there's no secret sauce, and everyone's journey is unique. However, there are steps you can take to accelerate your journey and save a considerable amount of time, money, and energy. You also must always remember what works for some may not fit everyone. You are truly unique and will write your own journey. Take all of this information and apply what you need to give yourself that added boost.

Remember, the definition of success varies based on who you ask. Ultimately, in your life, it's you who defines it. You're successful when you decide you are, and that word may carry a much different meaning for the person beside you. Numerous variables are out of your control, but you can position yourself to succeed in any circumstance. Align your goals with your definition of success so that, no matter the situation, you stay on your chosen path. Successful people practice the habits of success. That's what this book is about - not debating different definitions of success but helping you find yours.

When I started writing this, I began to examine my own path. What puts me among the seemingly "one in a million" who have enjoyed a lasting career in the dance industry, first performing, then teaching and choreographing, and now owning my own convention and competition?

Maybe I am lucky. Was I inherently talented? Was it all just a matter of being in the right place at the right time? Did I just have a really good agent? Was I just naturally flexible and found my niche? Is it the Cheetah

Mohawk? Yes, all of these things contributed to my personal success, but let me share the unadulterated truth. I've realized that luck played a very minimal role in it. To paraphrase Thomas Jefferson, the harder I work and the better habits I have, the luckier I get (I added "the better habits I have"). The most remarkable aspect is that my life doesn't feel like work. I'm currently living a life that far exceeds the dreams I had as a teenager. I have even bigger and loftier aspirations that keep evolving and growing, and it feels like I'm only just beginning. I'm experiencing a life of abundance. I am surrounded by a team of creative artists that are also really great people and I still feel the best is yet to come.

How did I reach this point? In my formative years, I wasn't the star of my dance studio, far from it. I didn't receive convention scholarships, nor did I win top competition solo awards as a teenager. No Mr. Dance titles. I wasn't born into privilege or handed easy opportunities. So, what's the secret? Well, for starters, I've been told I never stop "working." Some may even label me a bit of a workaholic, urging me to rest or take a vacation. I agree; on paper, it may seem like I'm constantly engaged in a whirlwind, but I always want to do more tomorrow. I've been told, "I know you must be busy," and I think no, I'm not because I'm in complete control of what that means to me. I love vacations but don't feel the need for a vacation from work because, in my eyes, my life and career are a vacation. I've arranged it this way; I'm in complete control of my own schedule. The things I love doing are seamlessly woven into the fabric of my life. People can be amazed by my daily productivity. I, in turn, am amazed by how little some people accomplish in a day. It's bewildering to me how they accept a cycle of unhappiness and dissatisfaction, day after day, year after year, without making any changes. In my experience, such individuals are usually the most negative and challenging to deal with. They lack motivation and are prone to whining and blaming others for their current position in life. This is more than likely because they're engaged in activities they don't want to do, often with minimal compensation and no recognition. It doesn't have to be this way. I've built a life and career around everything I love and continue to want to do. With the right habits and a little hard work, you will, too.

THE HARD TRUTHS

"You must want to be a butterfly so badly, you are willing to give up being a caterpillar." – Sekou Andrews.

Depending on your age and current situation, this book will resonate differently with you. Each person is on a unique life path, and where you currently stand will significantly impact how these principles apply to you. Your goals today should be significantly different from those you had five years ago and will have five years from now. If they remain unchanged, it is a problem that needs your attention. Like the above quote, you have to want it so much that you are willing to give up old, comfortable habits and embrace change.

What are you waiting for? Are you seeking permission to be great? I wish I could offer a magic potion, but honestly, only you can grant yourself that permission. You can wait for others to validate you or for someone to guide you with gradual steps and sound advice on why this path suits you. You can wait to win an award or get to the point where it's do or die to survive. However, why complicate it? Stop resisting the inevitable. There's no need for rationalization. Let these habits empower you to be great now.

It's possible to think a younger studio dancer aiming to win a competition or title has completely different goals and an easier ability to change their situation more quickly than someone preparing for college or entering the industry. You may think a current successful dancer has different objectives and is way further along than someone who is not booking and striving just to keep up. Let's face it: even if your situation and variables are different, we are all searching for the same thing: success. These habits are relevant for success in all situations. Use them as a guide, but know you will have to add your own ingredients. I believe that dancers often rise to the level of expectations and have an innate ability to quickly absorb the information they receive. This is why this book is intended for everyone, regardless of age, and it will reveal how you can keep progressing well beyond your current age or any perceived limitations.

If you are reading this and are merely hoping to survive, holding on to a dream while experiencing little or no success, and are still striving to catch your big break. That's ok. Things can easily change with a redirect of your priorities and habits. What's beautiful about these habits is that they can be applied to your unique situation, no matter what it may be. Be prepared, not scared. It's essential to be honest with yourself and muster the courage to confront the truth that, ultimately, it's you who determines your own standards. Are you "The One," or are you one of them? This book is for "The Ones." And that is a personal choice.

ASKING FOR A FRIEND...

During the first few weeks I started writing this book, I conducted an experimental survey to gauge the thoughts of others on these topics. One day, on a whim, I texted a group of successful friends and colleagues, individuals I would consider Prodigy Performers in the industry, and asked them to answer five questions. I kept it casual and mentioned, "I'm doing research for a book project... You can respond as briefly or expansively as you'd like." The respondents included professional dancers, choreographers, studio owners, teachers, and directors. I was interested in their responses, but I also observed their response times, response structure, and depth of answers. Essentially, what it turned into was that I was examining their habits in communication while simultaneously mining their wisdom. This shed a light on many important things.

I estimated that it would take a maximum of 5 or 10 minutes of thought to reply, which doesn't seem too much. These individuals are people I've worked with, for, or alongside, and I consider them friends and colleagues. I'd readily take a few minutes to assist any of them in a similar capacity. The response was overwhelmingly positive. However, I was quite surprised by certain other factors.

The time it took for them to reply, who responded instantly, who responded with, "I'll get back to you tomorrow," and whether or when they actually did. It was also intriguing to see who delved into philosophical discussions and who had difficulty answering the questions directly, often leading to more complex questions. For instance, one of my questions was, "What causes a developmental plateau?" One answer I received was, "A developmental plateau can be a positive thing as it gives dancers time to process." This interpretation, which views a plateau as the period required to transform new behaviors into habits, is a valid perspective. However, it doesn't directly answer my initial question. Knowing the personality of the person who replied to this and how I immediately judged the way they communicate was my first "aha" moment! This is what I found interesting. I responded to everyone with a simple "thank you." This was, after all, an unofficial survey.

After reviewing all the responses, I found that I could relate to all the answers on a personal level, even though the content varied. All answers were of a similar line of thinking. I next became even more intrigued by how these people I considered successful structured their responses. Some answered with complete thoughts and sentences, while others provided one-word responses, and a few responded in a somewhat nonchalant manner without delving deep into the questions. I even received multiple-page responses for each question from one individual. What caught my unexpected interest was the different and creative ways these successful individuals expressed similar ideas. Surprisingly, many expressed gratitude for my inquiry and noted that it made them contemplate their thoughts and served as a timely reminder. They wished me luck, commended the research, expressed excitement for my book, and eagerly anticipated reading it. Keep in mind that I only wrote, "I'm doing research for a book project." I must admit it heartened me that they all assumed I was writing the book. This level of support, even with minimal information, embodies the essence of Prodigy Performance habits. These people are aware that I wouldn't waste their time by asking if I wasn't serious. They practiced gratitude in their responses. They willingly gave time with the understanding that I completed what I started and that I enjoy developing creative projects and introducing new ideas into the mix. This realization was another "aha" moment for me personally. Over the years, my habits have evolved into a reputation as a Prodigy Performer; thus, I am treated accordingly. This changes how people communicate with me, thus changing every interaction I have with them and what I think of myself. Mind explosion!

This survey of people I respect also reinforced my understanding that sometimes it's not just what you say but the act of saying it and how you present it that truly matters most. In my dance classes, I often tell my students, "I don't want your audience to remember the steps you perform; I want them to remember the emotions they felt when you danced and that they want to watch you dance again." This philosophy readily extends beyond the realm of dance. Have you ever looked at something and thought "I don't know why I like it, I just do?" I don't remember the exact words used by many of these Prodigy Performers in their responses, I made notes and have summarized them for you, but what lingers is the fact that they responded, and I appreciated it, leaving me eager to engage further. The value of a simple reply cannot be underestimated.

This journey also served as a reminder to always allocate five minutes when someone asks for something simple from me. I may never fully grasp how it affects their perception of me and the impact it can have on their broader objectives. The responses I received reignited my passion to work harder and even though it took longer than expected and was more challenging than I thought it would be, through them, I now had the fire to finish this project and see it through to fruition. I was now held even more accountable, and I am determined not to disappoint. It's simply not in my nature. After all, I am a Prodigy Performer.

FIVE QUESTIONS

Here are the five questions I asked, along with a summary of the answers received:

1. Why do some dancers succeed quicker than others?

Answers from the Prodigy Performer Survey:

Success depends on factors like:

- natural talent
- a strong work ethic, having the right mindset
- resilience, desire, determination, setting clear intentions
- communication skills, being easy to work with,
- effective time management skills
- making connections
- recognizing personal wants and needs, maturity
- extreme passion and drive, self-accountability

- the ability to pick things up quickly
- kindness, the law of attraction
- being hungrier, strategic thinking, seeking extra opportunities
- positive parent or teacher influence, goal-setting
- timing, obsession, luck,
- quality training, technical proficiency, versatility, being prepared for success
- being in tune with one's purpose, curiosity, an open mind

2. What causes a developmental plateau?

Answer from the Prodigy Performer Survey:

Developmental plateaus can be attributed to factors like:

- settling for average, becoming too comfortable, complacency
- lack of confidence, fear of judgment
- puberty and growth spurts
- external influences pushing too hard or not enough
- excessive focus on social life
- loss of drive, running on autopilot, lack of goals and follow-through
- a lack of self-awareness, not listening to feedback

- body type and physical limitations
- ego, believing one has already reached the top
- poor quality teachers or classes, limiting oneself to one style or genre
- absence of competition, not being challenged enough
- needing a break or experiencing burnout
- lack of purpose
- injury
- overthinking, the perceived inability to progress

3. How can I stay positive and continuously motivated on my journey?

Answer from the Prodigy Performer Survey:

- maintaining positivity and continuous motivation involves personal choice, making it a necessity,
- defining your journey as part of one's character
- seeking variety and creativity, engaging with guest artists, and extra classes and conventions
- finding balance, exploring other creative activities
- allowing for feelings and emotions, discovering your passion
- setting and achieving goals
- surrounding yourself with uplifting individuals, expanding your sources of inspiration,

connecting with positive teachers, mentors, and influencers
- taking on challenges, accepting personal risks
- realizing that if you don't seize your time, someone else will
- researching history and finding inspiration in successful artists
- maintaining a safe environment for exploration
- starting a dance journal
- shifting focus from seeking recognition to personal growth
- dancing alongside the strongest dancer in the room
- reducing social media use
- understanding your personal sources of motivation and being excited about them
- embracing new experiences, changing your environment
- forming a dance family for social and emotional support
- ignoring external influences
- embracing rejection as a catalyst for improvement
- being authentic, honest, and true to oneself, remembering that you don't have to conform to someone else's expectations, and focusing on the personal payoff, allowing it to drive motivation.

4. How can I improve quicker and sustain that momentum?

Answer from the Prodigy Performer Survey:

To enhance your progress and maintain momentum, you can:

- set clear goals
- address your desires with concrete actions
- take care of your physical and mental well-being
- engage a motivational coach
- establish a strong training foundation
- maintain a consistent routine
- foster self-awareness
- embrace change
- practice self-discipline
- be prepared
- use success to propel further success
- engage in a variety of dance styles and techniques
- step out of your comfort zone
- develop a passion for learning
- coss-train with yoga or Pilates
- always leave the room as the most improved dancer

5. What are the three best habits?

Answer from the Prodigy Performer Survey:

The top three habits for success are:

- never giving up
- maintaining a strong work ethic
- being kind to oneself

Additional habits that were considered valuable include:

- consistency, focus
- knowing your "why"
- surrounding yourself with great people
- developing healthy lifestyle and dietary habits
- expressing gratitude
- punctuality
- strong mental health awareness and coping tools
- setting sincere and clear intentions, having a consistent routine
- embracing self-discipline, staying coachable, actively listening, and taking direction
- practicing daily affirmations
- keeping a dance journal
- letting go of the pursuit of perfection
- being prepared, conducting research
- holding oneself accountable

- respecting the values of others
- focusing on what can be controlled
- the "3 H's": Hungry, Humble, and Honest.

After reading all the texts and emails, one striking observation is how many people provided the same answers but to different questions. The same principles seemed to apply universally. Goal setting, a strong work ethic, and finding happiness and love in what you do were consistently at the forefront. All in all, it does not matter what order you put the ingredients in. They are the same. Everything is becoming clearer now, isn't it? Read the next part slowly in a studious Brittish accent please.

<u>With utmost confidence, we can now conclude that goal setting, a strong work ethic, and finding joy and passion in your pursuits are key to maintaining a positive outlook, sustaining motivation, making swift improvements, and breaking through developmental plateaus to achieve your dreams faster than others.</u> I might reiterate this more than once, in various ways in this book, so take a moment to read that last sentence again—it's lengthy but profoundly true. Now, let's delve deeper.

The primary aim of this book is to inspire and guide you on your journey. It's not about providing all the answers that worked for me and expecting you to replicate them to instantly become successful. That would be too easy, and life doesn't usually work that way. My hope is to nurture your ability to think independently and create new, remarkable pathways rather than merely copying those who came before you. I want you to discover your unique self and trust that you'll unearth the answers when you need them. Your journey is distinct from mine, and what works for me may not directly apply to you. I intend to reshape your perspective on questions and empower you to reframe challenges differently. I want you to plan, analyze, and develop the correct connections. I want you to soar further and faster, and I'm confident these habits will lay a robust foundation for your journey. This book should serve as a catalyst and guide to help you define what success means to you and set you on a positive path to achieve it.

SUGGESTIONS FOR GETTING THE MOST OUT OF THIS BOOK

•Tailor everything to align with your specific goals, creating a personalized learning experience. **It's all about you!**

• Don't hesitate to revisit passages when there's much to absorb. Revisiting passages and taking the time to fully comprehend the content enhances reading retention and ensures a solid grasp of the concepts. This meticulous approach to reading comprehension is crucial for applying the knowledge in this book and in life. **Read it again!**

• If necessary, take it slow. Close the book after each section, reflect upon it, and then return to address any lingering questions before moving forward. Allowing ideas to soak in and taking breaks between sections provides the mental space needed for reflection. This practice also ensures that you address any uncertainties or questions, reinforcing your understanding before proceeding further. **Let it simmer!**

• After finishing the book, circle back to the most impactful sections you loved, enabling you to reinforce the key takeaways and identify what is truly needed.

• Similarly, revisiting challenging sections ensures that you tackle areas of difficulty, dedicating additional time and effort to master complex topics. These are likely the aspects you can readily apply and are needed most.

Whatever you're currently experiencing in life, it's relevant today, in this moment. However, keep in mind that this will evolve over time. Comfortable journeys are rarely commonplace; if this path were easy, everyone would do it. Understand that it will be as manageable as you decide it is. Learn to embrace being uncomfortable. Some may argue that being successful is hard, but I would contend that not achieving your full potential is the greater challenge. Ultimately, it comes down to you—your mental fortitude, resilience, determination, and self-discipline will determine the outcome. What do you seek from your life and career? Your focus now revolves around nurturing your passion for dance through learning, personal discipline, and growth in life. This path is for Prodigies; this path is for you. I'm confident that once you're prepared you will easily Do more, Be more, and Have more.

Let's begin.

"If I accept you as you are, I make you worse; however, if I treat you as though you are what you are capable of becoming, I help you become that." - Johann Wolfgang von Goethe.

SECTION 1: WHY ME? WHAT IS A PRODIGY PERFORMER? AM I ONE?

If you're questioning whether a career in dance is the right path for you, you're not alone. There are thousands of dancers worldwide grappling with the same dilemma. If your answer is, "I don't know, or I'm not sure," then I'll be real – it probably isn't the right choice for you, at least not yet. I believe in being real, and unless you're ready to commit wholeheartedly and embrace a healthy obsession with your career path, it's more of a promising hobby with future potential than your true calling and chosen profession. While it's good to have options, I believe it's even better to thrive in precisely what you're passionate about. You might experience initial success by testing the waters before making a full commitment, but eventually, you must dive deep to determine whether the dance world is genuinely the right fit for you. This doesn't mean it's the only path you can ever follow, far from it, but, in my opinion, it requires an unwavering focus. Then, once you have all the success you want, change your mind! Refocus your path and find your success again. Do it over and over, and enjoy it!

The ultimate goal here is to discover your purpose. Remember, everything, including the inner voice in your head, is malleable. Your skill and talent aside, if you can't decide what your game is, how do you ever get in it, let alone play it? It's time to reflect. Once you've chosen that the dance industry is your path, it's time to decide in what capacity you will tackle it first and then take steps to make it happen. It's time to prepare your playbook and train. Then, when you're ready, the transition from training to a professional dancer will require an entirely different mindset that you will be ready for and will feel like a natural progression.

For most young dancers embarking on their journey toward a professional career, there can be a lack of understanding. Many believe that everything is on an extreme, either not achievable or instantaneous. I'm sure many have thought all they need is a love for dance, exceptional ability, and a move to Los Angeles or New York to start a career. Of course, add in reality show appearance and a few hundred thousand YouTube and Instagram followers and that may seem like the golden ticket, right? After all, they're fantastic dancers! They have been winning competition after competition since they were three years old, so it is the natural next step. Just show up and dance, right? "My mom and my dance teachers all say, "I'm the best; everyone loves me!" What could go wrong? I'll just do what I've always done.

I genuinely admire this optimism. That should indeed be the ultimate dream, and I sincerely hope it works out for you. It's not impossible. I'm sure that has worked for a select few, and we always aspire to be the outlier. TBH, I truly think it's best to embrace your boundless enthusiasm with thoughts like that, and now and then, it may indeed yield success. But if things don't progress rapidly, and you begin thinking the industry owes you because of your talent, that can be a significant misconception. In Los Angeles or New York, every dancer with an agent possesses a certain degree of talent; otherwise, they wouldn't even be in the room. Merely showing up and being a highly skilled dancer is no longer sufficient. Even if your journey begins smoothly and you start booking jobs quickly, how will you maintain that momentum? Knowing your purpose, staying true to your goals without giving up, and building the Prodigy Performance habits you're developing now are the keys to this longevity. They will keep you on course through the myriad twists and turns of your journey.

MINDSET CHECK - 8 QUESTIONS

Now, let's check where your current mindset is. Give yourself permission to provide honest yes or no answers to the following questions. Don't overthink, rationalize, or second-guess. Just read the following eight questions and answer with either "Yes" or "No."

- **Do you feel like you are destined for greatness?** YES / NO

Your answer is absolutely correct. Regardless of what you choose, remember that you hold the reins of your future, destiny, or fate. If you want more, you have the power to make it happen. The first step is to believe you are worthy and that greater things await you. You must genuinely feel that you're destined for greatness.

- **Are you someone who doesn't easily fit into current molds and struggles to accept the norm as an acceptable life or career?** YES / NO

This doesn't exclusively pertain to those who might be considered unconventional or odd. It applies to anyone who feels like they've been or could be slotted into a predefined role that doesn't resonate with them. If this question resonates with you, it's because you're meant for something more, something beyond the norm. It's time to embrace your authentic self and expand from there.

• **Do you have enormous dreams and aspirations?**
YES / NO

Compared to whom? If your dreams seem colossal in comparison to those of your friends or family, it's time to seek new friends and let your family know about your grand plans. Share your dreams with them, seek their support, and make it clear that you won't settle for anything less. Dreams are meant to be grandiose. Doing things your way and breaking free from accepted conventions is the new norm.

• **Have you ever been told to relax your standards, calm down on your expectations, or actually do less?**
YES / NO

People who offer such advice have likely given up on transcending their current position and can't fathom the level of intensity you bring to your endeavors. They're echoing the herd mentality, believing that what's suitable for the majority is suitable for all. Let them relax, calm down, and do less while you continue conquering your dreams. Not everyone follows the same rules, and you have the capacity to be bigger, bolder, and more in every conceivable way if that suits you.

• **Are you exceedingly competitive?** YES / NO

Embrace your competitive spirit! Stay honest and play with integrity, but choose yourself every time, especially when it's you versus someone else. The exhilaration of victory always surpasses the sting of defeat. Utilize your competitive nature to propel yourself and others to greater heights. Prodigy Performers don't compete to lose, particularly when their most formidable competition is themselves.

• **Can you hyper-focus and tune out unnecessary distractions?** YES / NO

Your ability to do this stems from your unyielding desire to accomplish the task at hand. You do this because you want it more than anything else. Refuse to let other people's issues sidetrack you from your goals. Let the naysayers and detractors talk while you go out and achieve. Conserve your energy for what truly propels you towards your objectives.

• **Are you more critical of yourself than others around you are?** YES / NO

Self-approval is the most vital aspect for Prodigy Performers. Are you obsessively driven by choice? Healthy obsessions by choice are the catalysts for greatness. You can love yourself while still holding yourself accountable. Self-discipline is imperative.

• **Are you willing to do whatever it takes to succeed, even if it means going beyond what others are willing to do?** YES / NO

This question is the crescendo. It encapsulates what makes you exceptional, what makes you extraordinary, and what makes you a Prodigy. Your willingness to work harder, longer, and smarter than anyone else is the distinguishing factor. It sets you apart from the rest.

Some may think that answering "yes" to any or all of these questions has a negative connotation. I would contend the opposite. Responding affirmatively to these questions is what will set you on the path to greatness. Coupled with the right habits, these traits allow you to channel your incredible energy into a career and a life filled with Prodigy Performance. It's time to pinpoint your obsessions and pour your time and energy into them without restraint. There's no more holding back; let your greatness shine. You are a Prodigy! Let's develop the habits that will enable you to perform like one.

What, exactly, defines a Prodigy Performer? The term "prodigy" refers to a person, often a young one, who possesses exceptional qualities or abilities. It signifies an individual who showcases talent beyond the ordinary course of nature, standing out as an impressive and remarkable example of a particular quality. If you consider yourself a dancer, all of these definitions should undeniably apply to you, and as a Prodigy Performer, they certainly will.

If you haven't yet acknowledged this truth, it's likely that the rest of the world hasn't either. After all, if you don't believe in your own greatness, why would anyone else? It's time to embrace the extraordinary power within you and channel it towards the realization of your aspirations. Notify the world, saying, "Hello world, I'm here to achieve greatness, and you'll undoubtedly love what I bring." Remember, you instruct people on how to treat you, how to perceive you, and what to anticipate from you. It's never too early or too late to recognize this and leverage it to your advantage. The following 8 Prodigy Performance Habits will revolutionize your life. Are you ready?

"Only postpone until tomorrow what you are willing to die having left undone." - Pablo Picasso.

Developing Prodigy Performance Habits

Developing The 8 Prodigy Performance Habits equips you with the skill sets needed to achieve long-term success in a variety of fields, not limited to dance alone. Prodigy Performers don't confine these habits to dance; they apply the confidence, experience, self-discipline, and leadership skills gained from these habits to every aspect of their lives and careers. Talent is essential, but knowing how to channel that talent, package it, and foster its growth with integrity is equally vital. Are you harnessing your talent to perform, create, and bring greatness out of yourself and others?

You've likely observed how people react to everything you do, from your verbal communication to your body language and even your physical presentation, such as your hair, makeup, and attire. Everyone responds differently, but the common thread is that they react to the impression you give them. You dictate how they perceive you, and the incredible thing is that you have complete control over it. The power lies in your ability to change any aspect you don't like at any given time. Change your habits, and you'll change your world. Once you begin implementing these habits, you'll never again settle for being seen, perceived, or known as anything less than a Prodigy Performer by your own choice.

While many dancers and athletes primarily focus on physical training, practicing these eight habits is what I believe truly separates the best from the rest at the highest levels. They are the key to achieving enduring success, both mentally and physically, as a person, not only as a dancer. These Prodigy Performance habits empower you to have more, do more, and be more.

Let's face it: Prodigy Performers outshine their peers in all areas of life. They handle stress, fatigue, and distractions better, consistently demonstrating resilience in the long term. Thriving under pressure, they deal with responsibility effectively, rebound from failures easily, relish challenges, and have unwavering confidence in achieving their goals, no matter what. They prioritize healthy eating, regular exercise, and sound sleep and lead happier lives. They earn more, travel more, and wholeheartedly enjoy their lives. By adhering to higher standards, you will become more admired, assume leadership roles, and possess a competitive edge in all areas. It all begins with the right mindset. Time to recognize that your success or failure hinges entirely on your efforts and abilities. You are in full control of your destiny. Everything is possible.

While traditional rewards are certainly appealing, Prodigy Performers develop an innate drive to work hard, not solely for rewards but because it defines who they are. Their habits are deliberate, infused with intent and purpose. They set objectives for every situation and are relentless in achieving them, never settling for less than their standards. They give the same great performance for an arena full of people as to themselves in the mirror. They work as hard when nobody is watching as when they are leading a room.

Prodigy Performers chart the course of their ambitious futures. They don't dwell on those they've surpassed or worry about bystanders on the sidelines watching their lives pass by. There's no time for rubbernecking. They maintain an unwavering focus on the road ahead, keeping their eyes fixed on the destination. It's all about the journey forward.

While Prodigies appreciate competition and value winning, their true competition is with themselves. They willingly forsake comfort and certainty for challenge and contribution. Over time, they envision a larger perspective, making external validation less crucial as they lead life according to their own plan, on their terms. Whether you already believe you're a Prodigy and aim to enhance your abilities or still need reassurance to make the leap, it's time to let go of any lingering self-doubt and take the steps necessary to fulfill your destiny. You are ready to be recognized as a Prodigy Performer and use these 8 Performance Habits as your guide to enduring success.

"Your net worth to the world is usually determined by what remains after your bad habits are subtracted from your good ones." -Benjamin Franklin.

WHY DO I NEED THESE HABITS?

The pursuit of truth is seldom comfortable or popular, yet it is profoundly rewarding. Many dancers grapple with uncertainty when it comes to advancing in their careers and making the right decisions for themselves, their families, and their future. They invest considerable effort, but the breakthrough they seek remains elusive. You have an undying love for dance, but what does that mean in the long run. Questions may linger about the true nature of long-term goals -what does "long-term" even entail? Is it one year, five years, or two decades? Many have grand aspirations for a dance career, but societal conditioning often paints these dreams as nearly unattainable. There's a widespread belief that dance and arts in general are merely a hobby, and "real" careers require a college education in more esteemed fields. That is complete BS!

For many dancers, their passion primarily lies in the actual art of dance and choreography, with little desire to engage in the challenging audition process or the social media game or to navigate the myriad hoops necessary for a successful career. These feelings are valid but may not align with the prospects of a flourishing dance career. All these factors can create confusion and perplexity. This is precisely why you need Prodigy Performance Habits. Utilize these tools to cut through the haze. These habits are applicable to any goal and any healthy obsession you can conceive. Listen to advice, absorb the insights of the experts, and then make your own decisions. There isn't a universal path to success. Even if you conclude that dance is not your calling, implementing these habits into any pursuit will unquestionably enhance your life. You are now in the business of YOU!

OUTSTANDING THINGS DON'T HAPPEN WITH AVERAGE EFFORT

In my dance classes, I often pose this question: "Why do a group of dancers attend the same dance studio, have the same teachers, and access the same opportunities for years, yet we see a range of outcomes—some are exceptional, some are average, and a few struggle to grasp it?" There are multiple answers to this question, primarily revolving around having the right mindset and a strong mental connection to what is being taught and practiced. However, the answer holds particular significance for those who find themselves on the end of the spectrum labeled as "struggling" or "below average." Those individuals might feel as though they've spent a decade without substantial progress, seemingly content with being average or even below. Not realizing the glitch in the matrix. This is what I hope is the "lightbulb moment."

For many, I think merely being part of the group and achieving slightly above average must be the ultimate goal. This, I believe, is unfortunate because they were never taught or never decided they were worth more. It's disheartening to imagine that the phrase "At least I'm not the worst" is considered a victory. Some are hesitant to embrace the possibility of judgment if they fail and, as a result, never fully immerse themselves. From now on, you are not one to shy away from challenges. You, my friend, are a Prodigy Performer, and settling for blending in or making no waves is no longer in your vocabulary.

I have witnesses many dancers content with surface-level engagement because that is all they have ever received, and they now lack the drive to deepen their understanding of technique and performance. They expend significant time repeating exercises without a genuine mental or emotional connection. Recognize the futility of this approach and understand that it will never yield the desired results. Transformation typically doesn't occur overnight, and your resolve will undoubtedly be tested. Prodigy Performance Habits will offer you a structured framework to stay on the right path.

YOU ARE THE EXCEPTION

Let's further complicate matters! The support and opinions of parents, teachers, friends and loved ones can vary dramatically, oscillating between "dance is merely a hobby" and "dance can be a viable career choice." Most often, these viewpoints stem from genuine love and concern for your well-being. As a parent, finding the right balance can be challenging. They may be trying to shield you from disappointment or find it difficult to relate because they've never stepped out of their own comfort zones. Be patient with them. It might sound harsh, but this process might be terrifying if they've settled for less, were unwilling or able to put in the work, or never pursued their own dreams. Usually, individuals who have trodden a similar path will be more empathetic to your journey. While numerous variables come into play, the bottom line is that they are hoping to save you from heartache, either by encouraging you to pursue an easier, average, and realistic life or one with goals and aspirations that do not fit your own -doctor, lawyer, or Neuroscientist. This distracts you from your path. Accepting mediocrity is just that—mediocre in any career path.

Say no to it, declare from the mountaintops, "I want what I want." Refuse to be shackled by the limitations imposed by external influences. Your duty and obligation are to surpass the previous generation. You either transcend, or you repeat. Be the person who sets a higher bar than ever before. Strive to go further and reach greater heights than your predecessors. You are the exception.

We've all heard the saying, "Hard work beats talent when talent doesn't work hard." It sounds appealing, but it's not always the full truth. Some dancers can rely on their looks, tricks, and raw talent and enjoy success. Unfortunately, that is usually only for a brief moment. This rarely sustains long-term success. A correct mindset and well-established Prodigy Performance habits are the real keys to triumph. You possess the ability to perform better and maintain consistency; it's right within your reach. You already understand how to motivate yourself. As a dancer, you have developed discipline and a robust work ethic, but you must assemble the right habits. Disregard the notion of life being fair; life is inherently unfair, and you must play the hand you're dealt. These habits will empower you to seize victory on your own terms.

HARD WORK ALONE ISN'T ENOUGH

"Thinking is the hardest work there is, which is probably the reason so few engage in it." - Henry Ford.

Hard work in a dance class can be an elusive concept to quantify. What one person finds incredibly challenging may be a breeze for another, and vice versa. Everyone possesses unique strengths and weaknesses, which adds complexity to the assessment of hard work. Things get even more complicated when all that hard work seems to yield minimal results.

Consider a level one ballet class: It can be either an incredibly rigorous challenge or a cakewalk, depending on your approach and what you aim to gain from it. This ballet class serves as a potent metaphor for both your dance career and life in general. Are you merely going through the motions, ticking boxes, and striving to get things done to make it through the day? Or are you genuinely learning, growing, and applying the knowledge you've been accumulating for years? In most classes, you know all the right technical corrections, so why don't you hold yourself to the same high standard outside of class? The fun in the class is the choreography style and emotion. These habits are the technique, and life adds all the other elements. The answer to that question is pertinent for most dancers.

Do you know any hardworking dancers who are still struggling to move up the ladder? They might be great people, apparently driven and passionate, yet they can't seem to break through, working diligently in class day after day but making little progress toward their dreams. You witness them putting in effort, and they manage to stay at a good level, but how do they transition from being good to being great? Is it as simple as practicing even more? Is that the answer? Should they be content with mediocrity and embrace where they are? Could it be that they've hit a wall and lack the inherent talent to progress further? What's holding them back? These individuals invest substantial time and energy, giving their all, but what if all their hard work and determination up until now was only sufficient to get them into the game, and now they need an extra push? Where can they find it? How do they maintain their motivation? How do they keep pushing themselves to reach the next level that seems perpetually out of reach while maintaining a healthy mindset and a positive attitude? This scenario presents numerous variables and several viable options to consider.

When hard work seems to be failing, it might be time to create your own opportunities. Flip the script. When you hit a wall, it's time to change your approach and make things happen for yourself. Sometimes, engaging in a new creative outlet can reignite your passion and help other aspects fall into place as well. Take new classes, experiment with choreography, host improvisation sessions, create concept videos, or do something new to stimulate your creative energy. You've probably heard the saying, "When it rains, it pours." Well, the same principle applies to success. Success begets more success. Return to your core purpose and tune out external distractions. Keep the energy flowing.

I don't just want you to surpass yesterday's performance; I want you to approach it differently. Give yourself a slew of new options. Brainstorm all the ideas and then pick what excites you. Some of these will feel excellent and yield promising results, while others may not. That's alright. Prodigies don't settle for what's reasonable. Reasonable and realistic goals often hinge on societal norms, values, and expectations, which may not work because they're based on past achievements, not the limits of human potential. Consider this: how could anyone else accurately gauge your potential and purpose? How could they possibly know what you're willing to settle for? Prodigy performers understand that they are meant to push the boundaries. Achieving this requires more than just hard work – it demands ideas, creativity, innovation, talent, intelligence, persistence, and determination. Hard work is a given; now, let's approach it with intellect and an experimental mindset.

When we get down to it, Prodigy performance is the result of adopting a set of practices that evolve into habits and eventually become an integral part of your character. Some of these habits might come naturally, and you might already be cultivating them, while others may require time and maturity to master. The question isn't whether you can do this but whether you will do it and when you will start. The key is to embrace the process and not only appreciate the results but also find fulfillment in the journey. I firmly believe that the only way to truly learn something is by doing it. By implementing and personalizing these Prodigy Performance habits, you'll reach new heights of success and effortlessly determine what is significant to you along the way. Now it's time to fly!

SECTION 2: 8 PRODIGY PERFORMANCE HABITS

THE 8 PRODIGY PERFORMANCE HABITS

1. The Correct Mindset
2. Proper Goal Setting & Planning
3. Clear Focus & Persistence
4. Healthy Eating & Sleeping Habits
5. Efficient Training/Practice & Dedication to Your Craft/Art
6. Highly Developed Social Skills & Presentation
7. Dealing Well with Failure and Setbacks
8. Confident Leadership Abilities

1. The Correct Mindset

Everything begins with having the right mindset. This is the most critical step and the first Performance habit. The Prodigy mindset begins with the belief that anything is possible and is grounded in the understanding that you are entirely in control of your thoughts and actions. What you put in is what you get out. This applies to every aspect of your life, whether it's in class, your career, your social life, or your personal and family life. How you perceive things shapes the direction and impact of everything you do. You choose what to do with both positive and negative thoughts. Your mindset is interconnected with everything. The importance of maintaining the correct mindset cannot be overstated. Our mindset, or the lens through which we view the world and ourselves, profoundly influences our decisions, actions, and reactions. With the right mindset, challenges are viewed not as insurmountable obstacles but as opportunities for growth and learning. It can mean the difference between giving up at the first sign of adversity or pushing forward with determination and grit. In both personal and professional spheres, cultivating the correct mindset is the foundation upon which success, innovation, and resilience are built.

Dance-related challenges are inevitable. A correct mindset empowers dancers to view challenges not as insurmountable obstacles but as stepping stones to growth. Whether it's conquering complex choreography or refining challenging techniques, a resilient mindset fosters a determination to persevere, turning setbacks into opportunities for improvement. Dancers with a growth mindset are more open to feedback, actively seek out new techniques, and remain lifelong students of their craft. This mindset not only propels dancers to new heights of proficiency but also infuses their work with a sense of perpetual evolution.

In the dance world, the significance of technical Mindset (attention to technique) is undeniable. However, nestled within the movements and pirouettes lies an underestimated force—the emotional power of mindset within your movement. Cultivating the correct movement mindset is the secret key that will unlock even more doors, enabling performers to transcend the mere execution of steps and embrace the artistry and soulful expression that dance truly embodies.

Dance is not a mere coordination of limbs; it is an intricate dialogue between the mind and body. A correct movement mindset establishes a profound connection between these two elements. Dancers who understand the intimate relationship between their thoughts and movements can harness this synergy to enhance their performance. Many Prodigy Performers use visualization techniques, where they envision flawless routines, enhancing muscle memory and creating a positive mental environment for success.

A Prodigy Performer's mindset also plays a pivotal role in exuding confidence and stage presence. A dancer with a positive mindset radiates assurance, captivating the audience with the sheer joy and confidence emanating from their every move. This self-belief is contagious, creating an immersive experience for both the dancer and the audience. Bridging the gap between art and entertainment.

Dance is an art form that thrives on vulnerability. To express genuine emotions through movement requires a willingness to expose one's true self. A correct mindset encourages dancers to embrace vulnerability, transcending the fear of judgment and criticism. By doing so, Prodigy Performers unlock the potential to create performances that resonate on a deeply emotional level, forging a genuine connection with their audience.

Mindset is truly the most important silent partner in every dance class, rehearsal, and performance, guiding the dancer through the intricate steps of both routine and personal development. It transforms dance from a mechanical exercise into a profound art form, where each movement is a reflection of the dancer's innermost thoughts and emotions. First step, get your mind right!

2. Proper Goal Setting & Planning

This habit enables you to create a clear path to reach your dreams. Proper goal setting and planning are pivotal to achieving success in any endeavor. Setting clear and measurable goals provides direction, motivates action, and serves as a benchmark against which progress can be evaluated. Beyond merely setting goals, comprehensive planning creates the roadmap to reach those aspirations. It allows you to anticipate potential challenges, allocate resources efficiently, and prioritize tasks. Whether it's perfecting a particular technique, increasing flexibility, or achieving a certain level of proficiency, clear goals make progress visible and measurable, allowing dancers to celebrate their achievements along the way. Planning ensures that actions are strategic and aligned with your objectives. In essence, while goals illuminate the destination, planning provides the route. Together, they form a synergistic approach that increases the likelihood of success, fosters accountability, and instills a sense of accomplishment upon realization.

Start with the most substantial goals you can envision, then break them down into smaller, manageable ones and map a course for ongoing success. You must determine the "who's," "how's," and "what's" for everything you wish to achieve. Develop a training and education plan for your dance journey. Chart a path. You may think you have all the time in the world, but in reality, your time is far more limited and important than you imagine.

It's essential to plan how you will train with those who offer the best chance of realizing your dreams. Spend time deciding how you can achieve this most efficiently. Know your ultimate goals within a specific, predetermined timeframe. Goals are not mere waypoints; they are glimpses into your future. By setting ambitious goals, Prodigy Performers cultivate a sense of vision that transcends the immediate horizon. This forward-looking perspective fuels ambition, encouraging them to dream bigger and reach for new artistic heights. Dance is a dynamic art form, constantly evolving with the times. Goals, too, must be adaptable. As you grow, so should your aspirations. Setting and revising goals with an eye toward personal and artistic growth ensures that Prodigy Performers remain relevant and engaged in their craft. Decide what you want and plan for it!

3. Clear Focus & Persistence

To execute the goal setting and planning of habit number two, you need habit number three—clear focus and persistence. Achieving your goals requires a sharp focus on them, as well as the unwavering determination to see them through. Your laser-like focus serves as the guiding light, illuminating the path forward amidst the myriad of distractions. It involves a deliberate concentration on the task at hand, allowing you to get the maximum meaning and mastery from each moment. Without this clear focus, distractions can easily derail your efforts, and when things don't proceed as planned or take longer than expected, persistence becomes your anchor. Paired with this focus, persistence is the force that propels one through the inevitable challenges and setbacks. Whether to give up or persist is a choice that rests solely with you. Without such targets, efforts can become dispersed, leading to decreased efficiency and effectiveness. Furthermore, clear focus and persistence will give you a sense of purpose and drive, propelling you forward even in the face of adversity. Together, clear focus and persistence form an duo that transforms aspirations into reality. Eyes on the prize!

4. Healthy Eating & Sleeping Habits

The health plan you establish to reach your goals must encompass habits one to three. As you can see, there's a clear progression in the 8 Prodigy Performance Habits. Healthy eating and sleeping habits are interconnected and are of utmost importance to overall well-being and optimal functioning. Nutritionally balanced diets fuel the body with essential vitamins, minerals, and nutrients required for daily activities, cognitive functions, and cellular regeneration. A well-nourished body is more equipped to combat diseases, manage stress, and maintain a balanced mood. As a dancer and athlete, your body is your instrument; this includes your brain, and both need the utmost care.

Proper nutrition and self-care allow your brain and body to thrive, positioning you for optimal performance. Maintaining control over these aspects can be one of the most challenging. Once you've defined your specific goals, it's time to determine how to put yourself in the best possible position to achieve them. This is a highly personal matter, and while the dance industry comprises various body types, you must decide what you're aiming for. An NFL lineman trains and eats differently than an Olympic sprinter, just as different dancers have their own unique demands. You must decide what product you want to present and take the necessary steps to embody that vision.

Sleep is often the last of these three habits to be addressed but is frequently the most crucial. It's when you recover both mentally and physically, and every function of your body depends on it. Sleep isn't just a passive state of rest; it's an active process during which the body repairs, detoxifies, and the mind consolidates memories and information. Adequate sleep enhances cognitive functions, emotional regulation, and decision-making capabilities. Chronic deprivation can lead to a slew of health issues, from weakened immunity and hormonal imbalances to increased susceptibility to illness. Inadequate sleep impairs your performance, both mentally and physically. Pay close attention and devise a sleep plan that aligns with your body's unique requirements.

Together, healthy eating and sleeping habits fortify the body and mind against external stress, promote longevity, and ensure that one's daily life is marked by clarity, energy, and vibrancy. Numerous trainers, life coaches, and dietitians are available to assist and educate you in these aspects. If you feel that guidance is necessary, I strongly recommend seeking their support. It could be one of the most important and worthwhile investments in your future you can make. Your body is your instrument!

5. Efficient Training/Practice & Dedication to Your Craft/Art

Performance habit number five involves practice and dedication to your craft. Habits one through four lay the foundation for how well you'll excel in this particular habit. Efficient training and unwavering dedication are the bedrock of mastery in any craft or art. Rather than simply investing time, it is the quality and focus of practice that distinguishes the good from the great.

Efficient training emphasizes deliberate practice, where one actively identifies weaknesses and works relentlessly to address them rather than merely repeating what is already known. This approach ensures continual growth and adaptability within the world of dance. It's not just class. It's the quality of class and what you take from it. Dedication to one's craft or art transcends mere practice; it embodies a deep emotional and psychological commitment, a passion that drives individuals to persevere even in the face of setbacks and challenges. It is this dedication that propels artists and professionals to push boundaries, innovate, and achieve excellence. In essence, while efficient training provides the tools and techniques, dedication infuses the soul and spirit, culminating in a harmonious blend of skill and passion that elevates one's work to remarkable heights. They work together, and one without the other is pointless.

Well-rounded, versatile training is essential, but honing in on your specific weaknesses is equally crucial. It's recommended to maintain a balance between variety and repetition to stay sharp in all styles. Pay special attention to what you excel at, as this is your niche and often what sets you apart from the rest while simultaneously developing and maintaining everything else. A well-defined niche provides a competitive edge in the crowded world of dance. It becomes what you can be known for, enabling one to carve out a distinct identity, cater to a specific audience or need, and establish oneself as an authority or go-to resource.

All five of these Performance habits are needed to truly be outstanding at any one of them. Having the right mindset, setting goals, planning effectively, staying focused, being persistent, adopting a healthy diet, and ensuring proper rest (practicing the first five habits) will allow you to undertake Habit number 5, efficient training. This inspires unwavering dedication from Prodigy Performers, perfecting their craft at the highest level. Once you make the mental shift from being an amateur to a professional, dance becomes your life, not only your job but your passion!

6. Highly Developed Social Skills & Presentation

Performance habit number six encompasses highly developed social skills and presentation. Even the best dancers in the world must be able to market themselves effectively and present a polished product. Strong social skills play a vital role in this process. Given that dance is a visual art, your presentation, both on and off the stage, significantly impacts how you are perceived as a person.

As a dancer, body language is important and is most often the first impression people have of you. Good body language is a silent yet powerful communicator, often speaking louder than words. It plays a pivotal role in how we present ourselves and how others perceive us. Positive body language, such as maintaining eye contact or standing tall with an open posture, exudes confidence and credibility. It can build trust, foster rapport, and facilitate smoother personal interactions. Conversely, negative or closed body language, like crossed arms, lack of eye contact, or slouching, can signal discomfort, disinterest, or even boredom. In professional dance settings, mastering the nuances of body language can influence the outcomes of auditions, meetings, negotiations, and performances. This is one way to never let your audience know you may have messed up the choreography or forgotten the moves. Many dancers give away their lack of confidence or happiness with how they just performed with poor body language. On a personal front, it aids in forming genuine connections and understanding the unspoken emotions or concerns of others. As much as we rely on verbal communication, it's crucial to recognize that our bodies often reveal our true feelings and intentions, making it imperative to cultivate awareness and mastery of this non-verbal language.

In today's world, your presentation includes your presence on social media. Of course, this subject is an entire book yet to be written. Pay close attention to market trends and make sure you are leveraging every possible platform to the fullest. People judge you based on your communication skills and the image you project. Exceptional social skills and the ability to communicate effectively on various levels can make all the difference. When people genuinely like you and feel they can communicate effectively with you, they are more inclined to want to work with you.

Your relationship with agencies, choreographers, directors, etc., is paramount. Many times, your final impression is what gets you asked back. While first impressions are undeniably influential, the significance of a strong final impression cannot be overlooked. The closing moments of an interaction, meeting, or experience often leave an enduring mark, shaping how the entire encounter is remembered and influencing future interactions. A positive final impression acts as a seal, consolidating the goodwill established and ensuring that one is remembered fondly. Follow up and thank them for the opportunity. Do your job... Make it look good!

7. Dealing Well with Failure and Setbacks

Failure is an integral part of life, and handling it with grace is the focus of habit number seven. Dealing with failures in dance is an art in itself, requiring resilience, introspection, and a commitment to continuous improvement. The lessons you derive from your failures guide and shape your journey. Understanding that failure is a temporary setback and having the ability to bounce back from adversity makes you resilient.

Whether it's in a dance class or an audition, Prodigy Performers view failures as both motivation and a gauge to identify areas that need improvement. Constructive feedback, even when pointing out shortcomings, is a valuable asset in the dancer's journey. Instead of shying away from criticism, dancers should actively seek constructive feedback from quality instructors, peers, and mentors. Honest assessments provide insights that can lead to breakthroughs, helping dancers address weaknesses and refine their skills.

Failure provides you with a roadmap to success. It's about acknowledging your shortcomings, learning from them, and moving forward. Many times, it's not the failure that is even remembered; rather, it's the recovery that is celebrated. Dance is an emotional and expressive art form, and failures can evoke a range of emotions. Rather than suppressing these emotions, Prodigy Performers can channel them into their artistry. Transforming setbacks into fuel for passionate performances, adding depth and authenticity to their expressions, and creating a richer connection with the audience. It's all connected, and practicing the first seven habits will equip you with everything needed to deal with any perceived failure or setback with grace and humility. With persistence, dedication, and a commitment to improvement, Prodigy Performers develop the ability to rewrite the narrative of their journey, turning failures into triumphant comebacks. The most mesmerizing performances often emerge from the ashes of temporary setbacks!

8. Confident Leadership Abilities

The final Performance habit is number eight, which centers on confident leadership abilities. Prodigy Performers are natural leaders and consistently display exceptional leadership skills, steering themselves and others toward successful outcomes in various situations. This habit is one of the most critical because it serves as the glue that binds everything together. The first seven habits naturally lead here. Leadership abilities are essential for Prodigies to consistently perform at the highest level and eliminate the element of chance.

A leader who exudes confidence not only stands firm in their convictions but also instills a sense of assurance and trustworthiness among followers. This self-assuredness is not about having all the answers but about having the courage to make decisions, take calculated risks, and assume accountability for outcomes. Confident leaders serve as beacons, especially in tumultuous times, offering direction and stability. Their self-belief motivates and uplifts team members, fostering an environment where individuals feel valued and empowered to contribute. It's worth noting that true leadership confidence is rooted in competence, experience, and continuous learning, distinguishing it from mere arrogance. By striking this balance, Prodigy Performers cultivate a culture of respect, innovation, and resilience, driving collective success and growth. Furthermore, it sets a higher standard for success and inspires everyone involved to reach that level. The confidence of a leader in handling whatever challenges arise resonates with everyone in the mix, and Prodigy Performers thrive in such situations.

Are you proactive or waiting to be told what to do? I love a person who walks into a room and instantly sees what they could do to make the room and everyone in it better. Being proactive means taking initiative, anticipating needs, and acting to address them even before being asked to do so. This is taking the lead, hence being a leader. Prodigy Performers are proactive and are often invaluable team members because they actively contribute to their environment, seek out solutions, and work to make things better.

Developing a proactive leadership mindset involves observing your surroundings, understanding the needs of the situation or the people around you, and taking action. It also requires a degree of confidence and the willingness to take responsibility for your actions, even if things don't go as planned. By being proactive, individuals can create positive changes in their environments and cultivate a reputation as a reliable, forward-thinking leader.

Is your mind spinning? Cheeks red? Motivated? It's time to think about how you will implement these eight habits. Take a few minutes to ponder how each one directly relates to your current situation. Undoubtedly, you already practice a few of them and probably have a few others that need some attention. Perfect! That's why you're reading this. Congratulations! You're remembering, learning, and implementing new things... Doing more, Being more, and that will lead to having more!

SECTION 3: WHAT'S HOLDING YOU BACK?

"The way to get started is to quit talking and begin doing."
- Walt Disney.

Now that you know the 8 Performance Prodigy Habits, there are likely countless answers to the question, "What's holding you back?" Many of these reasons probably involve external influences, such as friends, parents, teachers, studios, economic constraints, or geographical location. Each of these reasons has some validity to a certain extent. However, they are all challenges that can be overcome. These factors are variables, not constants. This means they are excuses. They can all be changed or, at the very least, addressed in a flexible manner. Some might be easier to address than others, but the point is to reach a stage where none of these factors serve as a valid excuse for holding you back.

The simple answer to the question "What's holding you back?" is, quite frankly, you are. When you decide not to accept "no" as an answer and trust that there's a path around all these external factors, you will find a way. When you begin practicing Prodigy Habits, you'll realize that the most significant thing holding you back all along has been yourself, coupled with a lack of attention to specific habits and the ability to think of a workaround.

The crucial thing to remember is that offering average effort yields average results. This principle applies to all facets of life. After considering physical dance-related excuses, such as being too tall, too short, too skinny, too overweight, having the wrong hair color or skin color, or being too old, and on and on, you decide what is needed to reach beyond uncontrollable factors and transcend that.

Now, what else is holding you back? A fantastic method for identifying these obstacles is to maintain a detailed daily journal. Much more on this later. Over the course of a few weeks and then months, you'll witness quantified and tracked data. This will help you see what's impacting your desired outcomes, what's missing, or what needs to be eliminated. Include aspects like sleep, nutrition, and training in addition to social and emotional challenges. Any and all insight on what is truthfully happening will raise awareness about the habits in which you excel and those you need to work on more diligently. It will reveal how you spend your time and energy, allowing you to make adjustments that align with your goals.

I'm consistently amazed at the number of dancers who are genuinely better than they give themselves credit for. However, they seem to lack confidence, struggle to accept praise, and fail to articulate the self-assuredness they should possess. These beautiful artists often lack basic social skills and follow-through in their business interactions. Their presentation skills don't align with their aspirations, or they can be virtually non-existent. They crave external validation but have no idea how to process it when they receive even the slightest positive reinforcement. This can be as frustrating for them as it is for those they interact with.

Being well-rounded is a crucial quality and can open up many more opportunities. In today's world of fusion styles, a versatile dancer who can adapt to various genres is incredibly valuable. However, it's equally important to find a niche or specialty—something you can master and become the go-to expert in. Many successful dancers have become known for excelling in a particular area, and then they use their versatility to surprise those who may have pigeonholed them.

The toughest but simplest solution to holding yourself back is three little words: "Get Over Yourself," and I mean this in the nicest way. Give yourself a break and go with the great flow you have created.

I'M NOT THE BEST DANCER IN THE ROOM

Being recognized as the top dancer in your studio or class doesn't hold much significance in the outside world but can change the way you are treated and the opportunities you are afforded within your bubble. For many, it's merely the first step in the inevitable rise to the top of every situation. For others, this is the first taste of success. If you are indeed that dancer, that's wonderful for your ego and competitive spirit, but now that you recognize this, it's time to broaden your horizons. This doesn't define you, and everyone cannot always be the proverbial favorite. Either way, challenge yourself to reach new heights. It's common to see dancers struggle when they find themselves no longer reigning supreme in a room. This can be influenced by subjective opinions and external pressures. They've grown so accustomed to being at the top that they've forgotten how to summon their best and what it took to reach that level in the first place. Complacency is a squandered opportunity.

So, why do some dancers achieve the extraordinary while others unwittingly block themselves from such prospects? Most likely, it's because they've been conditioned by their backgrounds and past experiences, as well as the influence of parents, teachers, and friends. They've been encouraged to aim for the status quo or just slightly above it so as not to disrupt the established norms. They've been told to blend in and follow the crowd to ensure that everyone progresses at the same pace. This allows for an easier studio life and less jealousy and drama from others. Unfortunately, many studios' can even promote this because it is much easier on their business bottom line. Making exceptions for a select few can be difficult for some who are not in that group. Therefore, keeping the masses happy may be holding you back. The problem with this approach for you is that most people will never put in the effort to be consistently exceptional, so you have to wait for them. By waiting for the crowd to catch up, you are imposing delays on your journey to fulfill your dreams. This is unacceptable; it is possibly time for a tough conversation. Achieving outstanding results necessitates extraordinary effort, and there's no reason to hold yourself back for the sake of others' comfort. It's time to hit the gas and not look back. This, too, is a choice, regardless of natural talent.

Many people will admit that their goals fall far short of their potential because the world or their own head has convinced them to set small, easily attainable goals to avoid the fear of failure. However, this only yields small, realistic results. It's time for that shift in mindset. What do you do when willpower, practice, and your innate abilities are insufficient to propel you to the next level? The answer: Prodigy Performance Habits. It's time to have more, do more, and be more.

AM I DOING TOO MUCH?

"It had long since come to my attention that people of accomplishment rarely sat back and let things happen to them. They went out and happened to things." -Leonardo Da Vinci.

This quote by Leonardo Da Vinci is truly inspiring! It serves as a reminder that you can accomplish more; you have the power to make things happen. It's time to break free from the constraints of external influences that are holding you back. Self-limitation in the quest not to disturb the status quo serves no purpose. Nobody ever says, "Dream small." Now is the moment to think on a grand scale to broaden your horizons. By this, I mean you should think expansively across all connected platforms in both your life and dance career, not just within the walls of the dance studio. You should think vertically, horizontally, and in all directions. Becoming a successful professional dancer involves more than just mastering dance technique and talent. Developing supplementary skills in various areas will enhance your overall performance and open doors to opportunities within the entertainment industry. Continuing to learn and grow will keep your creative spark alive and keep you relevant and in demand. The more diverse your skill set, the more you can contribute to any project. Learn at least the fundamentals of anything related to dance that comes to mind, whether it's lighting, photography, makeup, graphics, merchandising, music, editing, videography, web design, costume design, set design, business, and the list goes on.

Beware of those who suggest you're working too hard, urge you to take a break, or advise you to do less. They might be inadvertently holding you back. Naturally, there is a time for rest and rejuvenation, but truly exceptional people never do less. Resting or stepping aside to recharge allows you to do more; it doesn't imply doing less. Maintain this perspective.

How many of your favorite dance icons have you encountered who simply relaxed, did the minimum required, and ended up amazing, successful, and happy without having put in immense effort? The answer is likely none. Their journeys are typically filled with wild roller-coaster stories of trials, triumphs, and setbacks, but they never involve doing the bare minimum and waiting for success to come to them. Even if their diligence isn't always visible, you can be certain they've invested massive amounts of energy and effort behind the scenes, continually upping the ante and pushing their boundaries. Prodigy Performers have ever-evolving, loftier goals as they continue to achieve milestones. They don't believe in taking it easy. The obsession with excelling at what they love is a far more rewarding pursuit than any break or handout they could imagine.

I DON'T KNOW WHAT I WANT

"The trouble with not having a goal is that you can spend your life running up and down the field and never score."
- Bill Copeland.

"What Do You Want?" This is perhaps the most challenging yet crucial question you must ask yourself. You must determine your desires, or at the very least, what you wish to begin with. It's essential to dream bigger than you ever have before, especially if you consider yourself a Prodigy Performer, as your goals should be grander and more extravagant than those of your peers. The ability to dream big is the initial step. Following that, you must genuinely believe that you can attain these dreams. Craft a clear, bold, and concise vision of your long-term goals and connect them to your greater purpose. Don't hold back! Your goals should be substantial enough to maintain your focus and significant enough to dedicate all your efforts to. Your goals serve as the driving force for the actions you need to take. Ask yourself, "Do the goals I've set match my potential?" If not, raise the bar and then raise it even higher, continuously adjusting it for greater success.

The question, "What do I want?" should be ever-evolving, but you have to start somewhere. Begin by asking, "What do I want today?" This may seem basic, but you'll be surprised at how it can affect your life, not just finding the answer but knowing it. Be able to honestly say, "I know what I want today and have a clear path to achieve my dreams." Once you've determined this, always keep your focus on the future. Let your work be your teacher. With each step, you'll learn more about who you are and what you want to achieve. Celebrate your victories and move on to the next challenge. While you should savor the journey, remember that it's the destination you're striving for. Don't settle for a pleasant journey that never reaches its destination. Make it happen, and then book your next trip. Rinse and repeat.

Break down your wants, which are your goals, into small, manageable tiers with challenging yet realistic timelines. The challenging aspect is crucial because prodigy performers thrive under pressure, and setting short-term goals that are too modest can dampen your motivation. Keep in mind that some goals may require significantly more effort than anticipated. Don't be discouraged; extraordinary goals demand extraordinary effort. One of the most common mistakes people make is underestimating the time, effort, and resources needed to achieve their dreams. Instead of letting this discourage you, use it as an opportunity for precise planning and execution. On the other hand, some goals may seem to materialize more effortlessly than expected, providing an unexpected boost. What feels better: planning for more and something costing less time, energy, or money, or planning for less and it ends up costing more? Exactly. By adopting Prodigy Performance Habits, you will set yourself up for rewarding outcomes without even trying.

It's crucial to break down your goals into as many skill categories as you can think of and set deadlines for each one. This is a personal scale but can be as detailed as winning the next 20 minutes and then the 20 after that. This keeps you accountable and prevents wasted time and energy on futile endeavors that require continuous reevaluation. This should apply to both your dance-related skills and your career and life goals, not forgetting the social aspect. Studies have shown that a clear plan with deadlines that hold you accountable more than doubles the likelihood of achieving your goals. Enhanced clarity in all aspects is vital. Be able to articulate your desired outcomes clearly. State what you want, and then take concrete actions to achieve them. Be willing to ask questions, conduct research, and experiment; this process may not always have a simple answer and might take some time to figure out. It's better to invest time in a well-thought-out plan now than to waste time redoing things due to poor planning.

Details matter; "everything" is not an acceptable answer. You must be specific and then break down your goals into manageable components that you can conquer. Aim to have a long list of daily accomplishments and let those successes build upon each other. Maintain a tangible record, whether it's a written list or a visual representation, of checking off each and every item. Keep the momentum going, as positive momentum is your ally.

Recognize that, over time, circumstances will change, and you will need to adjust your plan for continued success. Embrace this fact, as it indicates that everything is working and you are growing and in control of your life. Welcome change; it signifies progress. Periodically step back to examine and ensure that the future you are working towards aligns with your true desires. If not, be prepared to pivot and reconfigure your path. Discover where you can make the most significant impact. This might not necessarily mean becoming the greatest dancer of all time; there are numerous avenues to pursue a long and fulfilling career in the dance and entertainment industry.

Take your moments to celebrate your achievements, but remember that resting on past accomplishments won't lead to future ones. One of the easiest traps to fall into is thinking, "Okay, I've made it." If you spend too much time basking in your past successes, you may neglect to pursue the next one. There will be time to reminisce when you write your memoir. Prodigy performers are in a constant state of growth and evolution. Success is now your priority, your duty. Continuous progression is not just desired; it's expected. Prodigy performers ask, "What matters most right now, and how can I surpass expectations?" This mindset is the surest way to distinguish yourself from the crowd, and it should always be your goal. Aim to overpromise and overdeliver.

HOW DO I LOOK?

"Dressing well is a form of good manners."- Tom Ford.

Presentation holds significant importance. It not only conveys self-confidence but, more crucially, self-worth. Despite the opinions of others, it's vital to feel good about yourself. Dress and present yourself in a manner that suits your objectives. Understand the character you are trying to portray and make a conscious effort to embody it. For choreographers and directors, few things are more disappointing than a talented dancer with a sloppy presentation. Remember your character's role and immerse yourself in it. When you know you look great and perfect for the role, it is much easier to release your ego and lose yourself in the performance. I guarantee this shift will take your dance performance to new heights.

Let's face it, folks, appearance does matter. While diversity is embraced more than ever in the dance industry today, the truth remains that sooner or later, you'll be evaluated based on your appearance. Every professional dancer can recount a time when they were typecast or didn't land a particular job due to a physical attribute. They may have been too tall, too short, too large, too small, had the wrong hair, the wrong ethnicity, and so on. They worked tirelessly and were arguably the best dancers in the room, but it didn't matter. The person next to them had blonde hair, was taller and shorter, wore pink, or resembled the director's niece... It could be anything. Often, it's entirely out of your control.

Some aspects of your appearance can be altered or improved, while others are truly beyond your control. The dance industry has come a long way in terms of accepting diverse shapes, sizes, colors, and more. However, the color of your hair, your height, your ethnicity, your build, and other factors may still determine whether you get a job or not. Don't take it personally if you don't fit the specific criteria they're looking for – it's just not a match. Your goal should be to find those who are looking for someone like you. Learn to accentuate your strengths in any given situation and use that self-assurance to overcome any perceived shortcomings. Make sure you understand your target audience and what will best satisfy them. You might even surprise them with your unique look and prove that you bring something special to the table. Classic beauty isn't usually the main focus; it's about presenting yourself in the best possible way. Your authentic self is more than enough. Make them want to hire YOU!

As long as Prodigies are aware that they worked to their full potential (most likely being one of the best dancers in the room), they can be content knowing that this gig simply wasn't meant for them. A select few can share the story of how they defied casting stereotypes, were undeniable, and got the role anyway. This is the goal and mindset of Prodigy Performers. If this opportunity isn't for me, it's okay; I'll move on to find the one that is. The person next to me is of no consequence or competition. There's enough room for everyone to succeed.

Here's a secret: everything is a construct. Every award, prize, contest, job—it's all part of a fabricated narrative. The most astounding part is that you are part of that construct. Just as a dance is choreographed, so is your life. What's truly remarkable is that you are the producer, director, choreographer, star of the show, and even a member of the crew. You decide which songs to dance to, which accents to emphasize, which emotions to draw from, who gets favorable lighting, who to cast or cut at auditions, and what costumes to wear. It's all a thrilling and grand production. You don't need anyone's permission to begin enjoying dance and living life on your terms. What you need is a plan that doesn't limit your potential or your dreams. As I mentioned before, it's absolutely acceptable to aspire for more. It's okay to be ambitious. It's okay to take pride in your success and enjoy it. You can cheer for others while knowing deep down that you are the best choice for the work. Rid yourself of limited thinking. Forget the saying, "Good things come to those who wait." Instead, remember that good things come to those who work diligently, position themselves for success, and never give up. Abundance of success is available to all, but you must be willing to seize it. It doesn't matter if the glass is half full or half empty if you are the one pouring the water. Prodigy Performance habits provide you with a blueprint that you can refer back to throughout your journey. It's all about engaging in these habits and experiencing improved results every time. Nothing is holding you back.

IT'S CLOSE ENOUGH

"Success is the sum of details." - Harvey S. Firestone.

Details matter, and not just in the choreography. Don't settle for close enough. Directors, choreographers, and fellow dancers want to collaborate with individuals they can trust and genuinely like. Keep in mind that you're playing the long game. The most successful people in this industry were once your age and level, and they reached their current status for a reason: they paid attention to detail. Details are the building blocks of excellence, underpinning the difference between mediocrity and mastery. Paying attention to the intricacies, whether in art or daily life, ensures thoroughness and precision. While grand visions guide direction and purpose, it's the meticulous attention to detail that brings those visions to fruition. Overlooking things or settling for close enough can lead to oversights that, while seemingly minor in isolation, can cumulatively derail larger objectives or diminish quality. A dedication to detail enhances credibility, elevates quality, and ensures the efficacy of outcomes. It's often in the details that innovation is born, problems are preempted, and excellence is achieved. Thus, valuing details is not just about dotting the i's and crossing the t's; it's about honoring the process, ensuring integrity, and striving for the pinnacle of accomplishment. Consistently delivering high-quality, detailed results builds trust and a strong reputation, whether in a professional setting, in rehearsal, in class, or in personal pursuits. "Close enough" can tarnish one's reputation and erode trust over time.

Use the experience of mentors who are keen to recognize these details to leap ahead and avoid replicating the mistakes that made their journey tougher. Do this by surrounding yourself with people who have lived or are living the life you aspire to, as you can learn more from them than you might think. Longevity in this industry is not a gift; it's something that's earned and continuously fought for. Assemble your squad wisely, pay attention to details, and grow and evolve together!

I CAN'T DO IT - NOBODY CARES WHY YOU FAILED

"I have not failed. I've just found 10,000 ways that won't work." - Thomas A. Edison.

With mistakes comes failure, and it is an inescapable facet of life. How you confront it defines your journey. Prodigy Performers swiftly transform failures into learning experiences, opportunities for a fresh start, and often catalysts for success. They don't dwell on their setbacks; instead, they derive motivation from them, sometimes even more than from their expected successes. Failure is synonymous with challenge, and challenge begets strength. Prodigies understand that failure is fleeting, and it fuels their determination to surmount obstacles. A positive mindset, combined with exceptional problem-solving skills and unwavering determination, ensures that they identify the cause of failure and develop a plan to conquer it. Turn your negatives into a positive.

• Didn't get that audition? **More time to train.**

• Get injured? **Needed a break from training.**

• Got beat? **Now have a better idea of what I need to work on.**

The character you reveal when you don't secure a spot motivates you to strive even harder for the next opportunity. If you're not encountering failure regularly, you're likely not dreaming ambitiously enough. However, it's essential to emphasize that failure isn't something to be desired; it's still an unwanted outcome and not to be settled for. Prodigies have a knack for converting negatives into positives, learning from their failures, and propelling their journey forward. Failures aren't what people remember when they think of iconic figures; instead, it's the resilience and ability to rise above those failures. Utilize your failures as stepping stones toward success and establish your legacy.

Handling failures effectively is crucial, but inviting them is not the objective. Turn your attention to studying and duplicating the successes of the greats, not the failed attempts. Your mission is to excel and make your performances truly outstanding. Acknowledge your setbacks, and then press forward. Prodigy Performers excel at overcoming these hurdles to realize their dreams. They're fully aware that the introduction of new elements can be seen as a risk because people often gravitate toward the familiar. Your role is to introduce fresh, creative ideas to the table. Remember, the most remarkable art is often the riskiest.

Have you noticed that some dancers always seem to have an excuse ready? It appears as though they invest more energy and effort into explaining why they couldn't succeed than they did in the actual pursuit of their goal. It was over before it started. This victim mentality is counterproductive and will never work in their favor. Blaming others or external factors won't resolve the issue. High achievers who practice Prodigy Performance habits in the dance world fight relentlessly for success. When things don't go their way, they understand that there's more work to be done. It's time to analyze, think critically, and apply their exceptional problem-solving skills. They know they will eventually find a solution; there is ample room for success. Excuses, however, serve no real purpose. It's tell the truth day! Nobody cares about why you failed, but they're intrigued by the story of how you overcame obstacles to succeed. The story of resilience and determination is what matters, not the excuse.

Dancers make excuses for a variety of reasons, often stemming from psychological, social, or situational factors. Here's a breakdown of some common reasons why people tend to make excuses:

• **Fear of Failure:** Avoiding Responsibility, Protection of Self-Esteem

• **Lack of Confidence:** Self-Doubt, Perfectionism

• **Procrastination:** Delaying Tasks, Lack of Motivation, Avoiding Consequences

• **Fear of Success:** Avoiding Attention, Fear of Change

• **Lack of Resources:** Time, Money

• **Externalization:** Blaming Others, Victim Mentality, Shifting Responsibility

• **Habit:** Learned Behavior, Social Modeling

• **Avoiding Discomfort:** Fear of Conflict, Avoiding Hard Work,

- **Lack of Clarity or Direction:** Uncertain Goals, Lack of Purpose.

- **Seeking Sympathy or Attention:** Desire for Compassion, Manipulation

Understanding and addressing the underlying reasons for making excuses can be the first step toward addressing them and fostering a more accountable, proactive approach to your challenges. If any of these reasons become habits, it's time to change them. Release the need for excuses. Accept what happens honestly and decide what you want to do about it.

For most, something as easy as a bit more effort can improve their results. This means that most of the excuses we give for not achieving our goals are, at best, just excuses and, more likely, simply wrong, or worse, in the eyes of a Prodigy, lazy. Relying on excuses won't change the situation. Prodigy Performers don't play the victim; they make things happen. They don't wait for things to fall into place; they take action. They don't plan to get just what they put in; they aim to achieve a return with interest. Constantly reassessing their Performance Habits allows Prodigies to do just that. Failing to live up to your potential is a conscious choice.

So, why do some dancers persistently try and fail while others hardly seem to make an effort at all? It's more than likely all in the perception. Have you seen the picture of an iceberg that shows what is seen on the surface and then how huge it is beneath it? Some people like to show their work. Others keep the struggle hidden far out of site.

DEALING WITH BURNOUT

For dancers who've spent 15 years growing up in a dance studio, there's been a considerable investment of blood, sweat, and tears. At some point, they might experience bouts of burnout, plateau, lose passion, or simply age out. This isn't necessarily a bad thing, and it happens every year at all studios. It's important to accept it and not to make excuses for them. It's not about judgment but rather about recognizing that they might have found that dance wasn't their true calling and they have other dreams to pursue. That's perfectly valid, and hopefully, they'll use the skills they've gained through dance to excel in their chosen field.

For others, burnout may result from putting in above-average effort while settling for mediocre results, poor teachers (excuse), subpar training (excuse), uninspiring goals (excuse), and a modest return on their investments (excuse). While they once aspired to achieve more through dance, they may have become uncertain about how to replicate or scale their success. Now, they're forced to settle for the memories of those few moments in their dance life when they truly excelled, if they ever did at all. Bitterness sets in, their confidence wanes, and they begin to question whether they have a future in the dance world. The structure that once supported their aspirations starts to crumble. This is when even more excuses enter the picture and, eventually, the decision to give up.

What we call "Burnout" is a state of physical, emotional, and mental exhaustion caused by prolonged stress and overwork. It can affect your productivity, energy levels, and overall well-being. Here are a few strategies to deal with burnout:

Identify the Source of Stress

• **Reflect on Causes:** Take time to think about what might be causing your burnout. Is it dance-related, personal, or a combination?

• **Seek Feedback:** Talk to friends, family, and teachers to get an outside perspective on what might be contributing to your stress.

Set Boundaries

• **Dance-Life Balance:** Establish clear boundaries between dance and personal time. Ensure you have time to relax and unwind.

• **Learn to Say No:** Don't overcommit. Learn to say no when you need to.

• **Vacation:** Consider taking a longer break or vacation to fully detach and recharge.

Prioritize Self-Care

- **Sleep:** Ensure you are getting enough quality sleep.

- **Exercise:** Engage in regular physical activity outside of normal dance class.

- **Healthy Eating:** Maintain a balanced and nutritious diet.

- **Mindfulness and Relaxation:** Practice mindfulness, meditation, or deep-breathing exercises.

Seek Social Support

- **Talk to Someone:** Don't isolate yourself. Share your feelings with trusted friends, family, and teachers.

- **Hobbies:** Dedicate time to other hobbies or activities that bring you joy.

- **Socializing:** Spend quality time with friends and family.

- **Professional Help:** If burnout is overwhelming, consider seeking help from a mental health professional.

Reevaluate and Set Realistic Goals

- **Assess Your Goals:** Are your goals realistic? Do they need to be adjusted?

- **Break Tasks into Smaller Steps:** Make large tasks more manageable by breaking them into smaller, achievable steps.

- **Time Management:** Learn effective time management skills to manage your workload.

Focus on What You Can Control

- **Control vs. Influence:** Distinguish between what you can control, what you can influence, and what is out of your control.

- **Positive Actions:** Focus on taking positive actions in areas that you can control or influence.

Find Meaning and Purpose

- **Reconnect with Your Why:** Remind yourself why you do what you do. What aspects of your dance life and regular life are most meaningful to you?

- **Volunteer Work:** Engaging in volunteer work or assisting younger dance classes can provide a sense of purpose and fulfillment. A great reminder of where we came from and also how far we come, and how much we have to offer.

Practice Gratitude

- **Gratitude Journal:** Keep a journal where you write down things you are grateful for each day.

- **Positive Reflection:** Regularly reflect on positive aspects of your dance life and everyday life outside of that.

Consider a Change

• **Environment Change:** Sometimes, changing the work environment or studio can make a significant difference. This does not have to mean leaving or changing your studio, but it can be adding some extra things to the mix.

Mindset Shift

• **Positive Thinking:** Cultivate a positive mindset.

• **Resilience Building:** Develop resilience to better cope with stress and adversity.

• **Acceptance:** Accept that you cannot control everything, and focus on what you can.

Dealing with dance burnout requires a holistic approach, addressing both the external stressors and your internal responses to them. It is important to be proactive and take steps to manage stress before it leads to burnout. No matter what your age, if you are struggling to cope, don't hesitate to seek professional support.

By the end of this book, my aim is for you to have no more need for excuses. You will be empowered with a set of habits that will help you achieve lasting, sustainable results. You'll learn how to continue growing consistently after your initial successes and feel confident in exhibiting Prodigy-level confidence, knowing that you have the ability to tackle any challenge – both mentally and physically. You're on the verge of understanding what it truly means to be a Prodigy Performer and how to utilize these habits to create the life and dance career of your dreams. Successful people engage in the habits of success. It's perfectly acceptable to Do More, Be More, and Have more.

SECTION 4: PROPER TRAINING

BE SAFE AND CAREFUL WITH YOUR TRAINING AND YOUR BODY

"Technique is what you fall back on when you run out of inspiration." – Rudolf Nureyev.

Many young dancers today are growing up in a spotlight where certainty is low, yet expectations are sky-high. We live in an era where it seems that dancers have been taught by social media to portray themselves as not working as hard as they actually are but rather as if they are naturally gifted with these incredible skills. The reality is that they are working harder than ever. The athleticism required for the skills dancers are attempting today is off the charts. I'm consistently amazed by what younger dancers can achieve. This generation is truly remarkable; the bar is being raised at an astonishing pace. Dancers are becoming more extraordinary at even younger ages, which has given rise to various issues.

Safe training is paramount in ensuring that dancers can pursue their physical, mental, and professional goals without undue risk. These protocols should prioritize your well-being to mitigate potential injuries and setbacks. It encompasses understanding one's limits, using appropriate warm-ups and exercises, and being guided by well-informed practices and techniques. Overexertion and incorrect technique can lead to acute injuries and even long-term damage. Safe training advocates for a measured, systematic approach, progressively building capacity while respecting the body's signals. Similarly, in both professional and educational settings, it emphasizes a balanced workload, proper guidance, and an environment conducive to learning without undue stress or pressure. In essence, safe training isn't about avoiding challenges but about engaging with them intelligently and sustainably, ensuring longevity and well-being.

Here are some key principles and practices to consider. Safe training practices are crucial for preventing injuries and ensuring a productive, sustainable dance career:

Proper Warm-Up

• **Increase Blood Flow:** Engage in light aerobic activity to increase your heart rate and blood flow to muscles.

• **Stretching:** Perform stretches to prepare your muscles and joints for the activity ahead.

Correct Technique

• **Technique:** Before performing complex movements, make sure you understand and can execute the proper form.

• **Use Mirrors:** Use mirrors to check your form or work with a teacher who can provide immediate feedback and corrections.

• **Start Slow:** If you're new to exercise or trying a new activity, start with lighter weights and lower intensity.

• **Progress Gradually:** Increase the intensity, duration, or volume of your workouts gradually over time.

• **Seek Professional Advice When Needed:** If you're unsure about how to perform an exercise or routine, consult with a teacher.

Stay Hydrated and Nourished

• **Drink Water:** Ensure you are adequately hydrated before, during, and after your workout.

• **Balanced Nutrition:** Consume a balanced diet to provide your body with the necessary nutrients for recovery and performance.

Listen to Your Body

• **Pay Attention to Pain**: Distinguish between the normal discomfort of a workout and pain that could indicate an injury.

• **Rest When Needed**: Give your body time to recover if you're feeling overly fatigued or sore.

• **Adequate Sleep**: Ensure you are getting enough sleep, as it is crucial for recovery.

• **Rest Days**: Include rest days in your training routine to allow your body to recover.

• **Balanced Routine**: Ensure your workout routine is balanced, including a mix of strength, flexibility, and cardiovascular training.

• **Signs of Overtraining**: Be aware of signs of overtraining, such as persistent fatigue, decreased performance, or frequent injuries, and adjust your routine accordingly.

Educate Yourself

• **Learn About Exercise Principles**: Understand basic exercise principles, such as the principles of overload, specificity, and progression.

• **Stay Informed**: Keep yourself informed about safe training practices and updates in exercise science pertaining to dance. You are an athlete; train like one.

Create a Safe Environment

• **Ensure Adequate Space:** Make sure you have enough space to perform exercises without risk of injury.

• **Minimize Distractions:** Reduce distractions in your training area to maintain focus on your training.

• **Medical Clearance:** If you have pre-existing medical conditions or have been inactive for a long period, seek medical clearance before starting any new program.

By following safe training practices, you can minimize your risk of injury, enhance your performance, and ensure a sustainable dance life. Like I said earlier, you are an athlete; train like one.

TAKE YOUR TIME

"Rome wasn't built in a day." -unknown.

It seems like these days, many dancers feel they can't afford to wait for proper training and instruction, and because there are no clear-cut rules, they're compelled to figure things out on their own to compete with their peers. They are now expected to just make it happen. This can take a toll on their mental and physical well-being. Performing many of these complex moves without the requisite strength and flexibility can lead to bad technical habits and long-term injuries. Simply being able to mimic the shapes doesn't necessarily mean you're doing an exercise or moving correctly. It's essential to be safe and cautious with your training and body. Trust me, the lack of attention to this leads to multiple knee surgeries and arthritis down the road. I'm living proof that what you're doing now may take a physical toll later in life.

As hard as it is for me (someone who is always quick to the next thing) to write this, The importance of taking one's time cannot be overstated. Amid the relentless pace of the modern world, where being fast and first often takes precedence, there lies profound wisdom in slowing down and savoring the nuances of each moment. Age and experience usually bring this to the forefront. Whether in the pursuit of personal growth, artistic endeavors like dance, or simply in navigating the complexities of relationships, Prodigy Performers know the deliberate act of taking one's time allows for a deeper understanding, thoughtful reflection, and a more nuanced approach. It is in these unhurried moments that creativity blossoms, relationships deepen, and the true essence of an experience is revealed. In dance, the deliberate execution of movements, the intentional exploration of emotions, and the patient refinement of technique all underscore the significance of taking one's time. It is a reminder that the journey is as important as the destination and that true mastery often emerges from unhurried dedication to the craft.

For most young dancers, the quick recognition you might receive from doing crazy tricks in competition or on social media will rapidly fade. Don't get me wrong; you should have all the fabulous tricks in your bag and use them with ease. They are most of the time necessary to stand out and be appreciated by many audiences, but the time and care you put into your training and preparation will be what earns you long-term respect from your audience and the dance industry as a whole. This builds longevity. Prodigy Performers understand that proper training enables your body to withstand the demands of a professional dance career. I'll say it one more time: you are a professional athlete, and you must train like one. Again, the willingness to do what others won't or can't is what sets you apart. So be smart, and please do it properly!

HOW DO YOU LEARN?

Mastering the Art of Learning Choreography and Achieving Excellence as a Dancer

Learning choreography effectively is a fundamental skill for dancers, and there are various learning styles to choose from. Identifying the methods that work best for you is crucial to enhance your efficiency as a dancer. It's essential to be adaptable, considering factors like time, space, and the particular teacher. Develop your own shortcuts and communicate your preferences clearly to put yourself in the best position for success.

• **Visual/Spatial:** These learners benefit from watching the choreography. They often need a clear visual representation, such as a demonstration by an instructor or a video. Their minds create a mental image of the choreography, which they can then replicate.

• **Auditory/Musical:** For these individuals, the music is their guide. They anchor their movements to specific beats, rhythms, or melodies. They might associate a certain step with a particular musical note or phrase, allowing them to synchronize seamlessly with the tune.

• **Auditory/Verbal:** These learners excel when they can hear the counts or specific verbal cues. The spoken word, whether it's "1, 2, 3, 4" or "step, turn, jump, land," helps them coordinate and sequence their movements.

• **Physical/Kinesthetic:** "Learning by doing" is the mantra of these individuals. They might struggle with just watching or hearing; they need to move their bodies, feel the steps, and understand the choreography through muscle memory.

• **Logical/Mathematical:** For these learners, dance or movement becomes a puzzle to solve or a problem to work through. They might break down choreography into patterns, sequences, or structures, understanding the logic behind every step and transition.

Recognizing and catering to these diverse learning styles is crucial for instructors and coaches. It ensures that each individual, regardless of their preferred mode of learning, can grasp, enjoy, and excel in their chosen discipline. Prodigy Performers are open to exploring alternative avenues, adapting to various styles, and cultivating a versatile skill set that extends beyond traditional frameworks. With that said, communication on this front is critical. When it comes down to it, make sure your choreographers, directors, and mentors know how you learn and are helping you get what you need to thrive. This will not only help your cause but make their lives easier as well.

FIND THE RIGHT HELP

You must take the time to acknowledge what you know and be honest about what you don't. Dancers are often told to ask questions but not too many, and they shouldn't expect instructors to take the time in class to explain the answers. Even that sentence can be confusing, right?

The key to expanding your knowledge and training is being able to efficiently ask the right questions. This is where "know your history" comes into play. Do your research; Prodigy Performers are keenly aware of who's who in the industry and where to find the information they need. Go to the best training sources. Identify who is an expert in the area you want to learn more about and educate yourself. Working with the right choreographers, collaborators, and team members enhances your overall performance and will transcend your individual capabilities. This knowledge also helps Prodigy Performers understand what's currently in demand in the dance industry. The more you know going into a situation, the better you can navigate it. In dance, as in life, a seasoned mentor provides valuable insights, constructive feedback, and a roadmap for growth. Their wisdom not only accelerates the learning curve but will also help you avoid potential pitfalls.

Align your training goals with other complementary goals so they work together to boost each other. Everyone's journey is unique, and the right help should be tailored to your individual needs with each step a strategic move towards success. Personalized guidance acknowledges strengths, addresses weaknesses, and facilitates a customized approach to growth. Whether it's adapting dance techniques to suit your style or receiving personalized advice for life decisions, tailored support is invaluable. Link them in a way that creates a synergy, where each smaller goal contributes to your broader objectives and builds momentum toward them. This will allow you to celebrate your smaller victories and maintain motivation. The rewards are built into the plan. This approach enables you to multitask while maintaining a laser focus on your desired outcomes in the dance of life, where every step matters.

SECTION 5: PRODIGY PERFORMERS EXPECT TO WIN

"I'll do whatever it takes to win games, whether it's sitting on a bench waving a towel, handing a cup of water to a teammate, or hitting the game-winning shot." - Kobe Bryant.

Do you consider this dance life of yours a competition or a showcase? I think it's both, and guess what – it's perfectly okay to win. Contrary to what you might have been told, winning is actually a good thing. Somewhere along the way, in the name of politeness, society seems to have made people feel guilty about winning. In my humble opinion, that's complete nonsense! We're encouraged to be the best and put in our utmost effort to win, only to be asked to act like it doesn't matter that much and that we are just blessed to be standing here. This is why I'm not a fan of the everyone gets a participation trophy crowd. You are expected to participate! (Hopefully) Nobody forced you; you signed up for this.

If you've ever been told, "Winning isn't everything," I'd agree, but I'd add that it's "the only thing" **when you're competing**. When you're in a competition, it's with the intent to win. Use every resource at your disposal, have integrity and honor, and don't hold back. You're a Prodigy Performer; I'm giving you permission to excel, to fully and completely outperform your competition, and afterward, to graciously acknowledge your efforts with a smile and a handshake and feel proud of your performance.

Now, guess what? It's also okay to lose. There's honor in defeat and motivation to be found in it. Embrace that sting and use the disappointment to refocus your energy.

Without winning or losing, it's not a competition; it's merely an exhibition or showcase. When it is a competition, Prodigy Performers expect to win. They utilize every ethical means at their disposal to ensure victory before they even agree to compete. Sometimes, this doesn't happen overnight, but for Prodigies, it's inevitable because, for them, there is no other option. They learn from each loss and use it as fuel to push even harder for the next opportunity to compete. Once they achieve victory, they're gracious, share the love, and eagerly move on to chase the thrill and excitement of the next victory.

Imagine a world where everyone adopts these habits and strives to perform at a Prodigy level – this could be the new normal. People would demand and expect more from themselves and others. Given the incredible capacity of human beings, I firmly believe we could rise to the occasion. It's happened before throughout history. Can you envision how quickly the world could once again level up and become a better place? This already happens on a smaller scale all the time. One by one, individuals set new standards and achieve more. The problem is that many people are simply afraid of this change; they don't want to work harder and are oblivious to how inefficiently they've been living. They've been conditioned to crave mediocrity and to be comfortable and small, content with whatever is available. Meanwhile, elsewhere, someone else has decided to do whatever it takes to excel, to work harder, and to create new and greater opportunities for themselves.

Even if they are not aware of the negative impact it has on our youth, many adults are perpetuating this average way of thinking. They condition generations to sit quietly and fall in line with the way things have always been simply because it's easier, considered nicer, or more polite. Let's be honest; it is less work. Prodigies refuse to settle for a "go along with the herd" mentality. Prodigy Performers want and need more. You want and need more, and it's time to seize it. Yes, it may take time. You may get your feelings hurt. You might not be good enough yet. You may lose or fail multiple times. You may get knocked down, tumbled around, and may question if all the work is worth it. The answer is an emphatic yes! That inevitable WIN changes everything. Overcoming a once-immovable obstacle instills a profound sense of accomplishment and empowerment. It's a testament to one's resilience, determination, and growth. When faced with challenges, doubt and uncertainty can cloud judgment, making things seem insurmountable. Yet, as one perseveres, adapts, and eventually overcomes, there is an exhilarating surge of triumph, often accompanied by a newfound confidence in one's abilities. They are winners and now have the mindset of a winner. This journey from apprehension to achievement not only strengthens character but also deepens self-awareness. It offers insights into personal strengths, areas of growth, and the strategies that work best when confronting adversity. This is why we compete! Moreover, the emotional tapestry felt during this journey – from initial frustration to eventual elation – creates a lasting memory, serving as both a reminder of what we are capable of and a source of motivation for future challenges.

EVERYBODY GETS A TROPHY

"When we give a trophy to every child, regardless of effort or achievement, we are doing them no favors. When rewards are tied to nothing, they are worth nothing." – Dr. Madeline Levine.

We live in a time when everybody gets a trophy but is yet to win; the bar is higher than ever. You still have to be the best, but others may get random trophies, too, and it may seem the whole system is designed so everyone has hope and doesn't feel bad. Even if you work hard and do win, odds are you are told you should only enjoy it for a short time and rarely openly. You wouldn't want to be thought of as conceited, and you definitely don't want to put yourself in a better category than anyone else, right?

This is confusing at any age for all parties involved. I have a definite belief in recognizing true achievement rather than mere participation. However, it's worth noting that the debate around participation trophies is multi-faceted, with some arguing they boost self-esteem and encourage better participation, while others believe they don't teach kids about real-world competition and the value of true achievement. The "everybody gets a trophy" phrase is now symbolic of these larger discussions about recognition, merit, and the values being imparted to younger generations. I'll let others fight that one out. Let's think of it as what works for us. As a Prodigy Performer, Winning works!

Although I fall on the side of the wins must be earned coin, when it gets down to it, none of that even matters. People who waste time worrying too much about the competition can never be fully focused. How can you be 100% focused on being great if you are constantly looking over your shoulder, wondering, or even caring if you have a triple platinum pin? Acknowledge what is happening and move on. Know where you rank with others your age and ability and make sure you know where you stand in the industry. A healthy competition with yourself will bring you all the wins you will ever want or need. Constantly looking over to see what the person next to you is doing is pointless. Decide what you want out of a situation, and worry about yourself and what you can control. The only thing that matters is that you continue to improve and are happy with your performance. Did you feel strong, and are you happy? Everything else will take care of itself.

There is a constant struggle for young dancers told to hurry up, be amazing, and wait their turn at the same time. I see this all the time, and it can be daunting and exhausting to even the strongest and best-trained minds and bodies out there. "I'm the top of my class, age group, etc., what now?" I cannot imagine the feeling of peaking at ten years old. What now? How do you deal with all this and live your best life, while waiting years to age into the next phase and eventually still be engaged enough to embark on a long and fulfilling dance career? When enjoying early success, how do you continue to climb higher mountains at any age while staying positive and enjoying the journey? How do you push past the usual hard work to stay at the top? Passion alone will not cut it. More practice? Sure, you're still technically great. What's needed is Prodigy Performance habits. This is the difference maker. This is what will set you up for the long term and keep you focused and on the right path.

For some, receiving the "Big Prize" or landing their "Dream Job" is the validation they seek in their dance careers. However, they soon realize that this kind of validation means little once that's over. It's an all-or-nothing mentality, and when it's gone, they feel lost. Regrettably, this way of thinking will cause you to miss out on the most rewarding aspects of the dance world: the joy of the journey, the validation of your dedication to your craft, and the satisfaction of practicing it and sharing it with the world. Every one of the Prodigy Performance habits complements the person you are, the reasons you love to dance, and the endless possibilities available to you. Everything is interconnected. Stop holding yourself back by comparing your abilities to others.

EVERYTHING IS CONNECTED

"Do not go where the path may lead; go instead where there is no path and leave a trail." - Ralph Waldo Emerson.

Now is the time to make the industry connections and build the relationships you will use when you are ready and able to make the next leap. Now is the time to expand your horizons and add as many "books" to your shelf as possible. Setting a plan in motion and being patient will yield great results. This is your "WIN".

Remember, we are playing the long game here. Want to work with people you like, people you trust? Guess what? Choreographers, Directors, and Agents are no different. Opportunity may originally be awarded through sheer talent or earned through rocking out a combination at an audition, but the relationships formed after that moment are what gets you in the club. That is your next "WIN."

It's true what you've heard, cliques are a thing. Many choreographers have a team they like to use over and over. More professional jobs are gained by referrals and repeat booking than by auditioning. This is the goal. Be on everyone's "favorites" list. Prodigies are amazing people who are trusted and back it up dance-wise. The dance world is small; everyone knows everyone. I can assure you that people talk. Repeatedly working with certain Choreographers can make your entire career, as well as get you booked by others because of the respect they have for that certain person's work ethic. It's all connected. Find out who those people are and find a way to put yourself in front of them; take their classes so you know what to expect from them at an audition and how it may be to work for them. Introduce yourself, communicate, let them know you are a fan, and expect to work for them one day. Not pushy but confident. Make it a goal for them to know your name when they see your face. Give yourself the most advantages possible; by human nature, your eyes go to what you recognize. If they already know you, they will give you that few extra seconds that may be just what you need to book the job. Then, make a plan for how you will stand next to them, compete for jobs amongst them, and maybe even eventually hire them for that huge production you have conceived. We are dreaming big, right? It's all connected. #Winning

WHAT MATTERS

"A girl should be two things: who and what she wants." - Coco Chanel.

What matters is you. You are your number one priority. You must take care of yourself first before you can take care of anyone else. Opinions of others are ultimately inconsequential, right or wrong, what you think is currently what's important. Now is not the time to be lazy about career decisions; you have the ability to do what you want and what is best for you because you are in complete control now. Your thoughts and actions will manifest whatever you desire to make it happen. Making yourself proud is your goal.

What matters is you. Get rid of any negative influences; this includes people. Stop wasting time on trivial things that are not bringing you joy and helping you reach your goals. Prodigy Performers must be disciplined. You have no time for other people's issues or excuses. Your focus must be 100% on what you want. What matters is you. Trying to explain or convince others of your dreams is really not necessary. Even if they think they are wild and unreachable, people will either support you or not. There is no need to beg someone to believe in you. Make it easy for them. Either you are for me or against me; there is no need for you in the middle.

What matters is you. Let people call you selfish. Pay them no attention. Those are the same people who will also claim to know you once you are enjoying all your success. They may pretend at first to be surprised by your continued success and think you "got lucky," but you should not be surprised at all. This is what you have been working for. Once you demonstrate it time and again, they will have no choice but to give it up for you. You, of course, knew it all along and would not settle for anything else. Being true to your wants and needs is what matters most.

What matters next is your purpose. This is what you have known you were destined for all along. This is what you constantly put your energy into, what feels good and right. This is your chosen obsession. The reason you exist. The what and the why. Dive into this answer with everything you've got and believe in yourself. Remind yourself of your purpose often. This is what will get you through tough times.

Now that you are in tune with what matters (YOU) drop the things that don't matter. No matter what your connection to them is, if they are not serving your current goals, then you do not need them. Release them and truly focus on you. You alone know your personal capabilities better than anyone else. Listen to your inner voice and live up to the potential you see in yourself. Prodigy Performance is not beholden to anything, i.e., race, economic background, or a specific type of person. It is about developing and practicing high-level personal habits. You decide when to implement them and are in complete control of them. There is nothing left to chance, and when followed, success over the long term is the only possible outcome. You are judged by how you communicate, and Prodigy Performance habits allow you the confident ability to communicate successfully on every level. What matters most is that you put these eight Performance Habits into practice and continue to review them. You must tune out all the outside noise, the haters, the naysayers, the people who are holding you back, and charge forward with everything you've got. This is your life. You must take control. It may not be easy at first, but remember all of these practices can be replicated in all aspects of your life. The more you practice them, over time, they will become a part of your character. Common sense is not that common! Many of these things you have heard before may seem like common sense, but very few people are able to consistently demonstrate these traits over the long term. The ones who do are Prodigy Performers.

SECTION 6: PRODIGY PERFORMANCE

Let's have some fun. Time for the interactive part of the book. Grab a pen and please answer the following questions for each aspect of your life. First, reflect on your personal life in general. Then, separately, focus on your life as a dancer, considering your current level and career status. It's helpful to jot down your responses in a notebook or on your preferred device. This practice will provide you with a valuable record to look back on. These answers will illuminate your current position on your journey. I recommend doing this now before proceeding to the next section. When you finish this book, revisit your answers to see if anything has changed. Make this a routine activity in your life. It's crucial to track your growth and identify areas where you may need improvement. This self-honesty will enable you to adjust your plans promptly and make progress.

Make a special effort to be candid with yourself, allowing both positive and negative responses. This is the only way to gain the true benefits of this exercise. Some questions may be easier to answer than others, and this will evolve over time. Your answers may overlap between your personal and dance aspects, or they may differ significantly. That's perfectly fine. The key is that having no answer is the only wrong answer. Remember, this exercise is for your personal growth and a reminder of your chosen path. Revisit your goals frequently to fuel your enthusiasm and motivation for self-improvement. Strive for more, do more, and become more!

Fun Fact: There are 44 of them cause 4+4=8, and by implementing and practicing the 8 Prodigy Performance habits, you will soon answer them all with ease.

44 QUESTIONS TO REFLECT ON PERSONALLY AND AS A DANCER

Character

1. How do I want people who don't know me to perceive me?

2. Who do I want to be known as to my friends and family?

3. What is my life's purpose?

4. What are my core values?

5. What are my strengths and weaknesses?

6. How do I handle rejection?

7. Am I setting a good example for others?

Motivation

8. What ignites my inner drive?

9. How do I generate my own motivation and energy?

10. What truly brings me happiness?

11. How do I stay motivated when faced with obstacles?

12. What propels me beyond those around me?

13. Are my aspirations as grand as my potential?

14. Who are the three individuals that inspire and motivate me?

Necessity

15. What standards have I set for myself?

16. Why is consistent excellence a must for me?

17. What are my limits, and where do I draw the line?

18. What responsibilities do I bear in my life and pursuits?

19. What has pushed me harder than anything else?

Focus

20. How can I maintain unwavering focus and minimize distractions?

21. What strategies do I employ to keep myself in check?

22. What external factors influence my decisions?

23. How do I acquire new knowledge and skills?

Plan

24. What are my specific goals?

25. Which goal am I closest to achieving?

26. What strategies do I employ to achieve both short-term and long-term objectives?

27. What immediate actions can improve my current situation?

28. What steps can enhance my long-term prospects?

29. How can I leverage my strengths to my advantage?

30. Am I effectively managing my time?

Support

31. What is my support network, and who are the people I rely on?

32. Who do I aspire to be associated with in my journey?

33. Who serves as my mentors and guides?

34. Do I provide myself with the necessary mental support?

Action

35. What consistent actions will I take to ensure I meet my goals?

36. Am I consistently putting in above-average effort?

37. Am I capitalizing on my strengths in my pursuits?

38. Am I committed to continuous growth and personal development?

39. Do I prioritize regular rest and recovery?

Enjoyment

40. Am I currently enjoying my life and its various aspects?

41. How will I celebrate my achievements along the way?

42. What is my long-term plan for deriving joy from life?

43. How will realizing my dreams enhance my overall life satisfaction?

44. What would bring me the most happiness at this very moment?

SECTION 7: ENERGY AND ACTIONS

"The dream is free. The hustle is sold separately." -Tyrese Gibson.

ALL THE FEELS

When approaching any situation, prodigies pose two fundamental questions: "How does this make me feel?" and "What feeling do I want to derive from it?" These questions are distinct but equally important, as they don't always align. Dance, more than any other art form, is deeply intertwined with emotions. Does dancing bring you joy? What about all the factors that contribute to this experience: the training, dieting, travel, and rehearsals? Is it all worth the reward? These are questions you must answer for yourself. From my own experience, the answers fluctuate, but I've learned to navigate this terrain as best as I can. I make it a point to place myself and those around me in the best possible circumstances to relish the journey and feel content about the outcomes of any project I engage in.

A dancer's role is to convey the emotions of the music and narrate a story through their movements. The feelings that the audience hopefully experiences are a collective creation formed by the music, choreographer, and dancer. These are typically deliberate choices, and these same choices are at your disposal in every facet of your life. It's up to you to approach things from various angles, sometimes collaborate, and steer them in the direction you desire. Just as you select how to perform and which emotions to convey when you dance to elicit a specific response from your audience, you can also opt for actions that yield desired reactions in real life. Just as you can execute dance steps and create shapes without a purpose, you can also move through life with no intention and little emotion.

The majority of emotions we experience in life are automatic and physical; I'm not referring to those. When I mention "feelings," I'm alluding to the emotions you convey to others through your words and actions. Non-dancers tend to be more verbally self-aware but may not be as in tune with their physical presence. For dancers, it's often the reverse. We are typically aware of ourselves physically, especially while dancing, but many dancers clearly are not as in touch with themselves in the outside world. We've all heard the saying, "body language speaks volumes," and it holds true. How you carry yourself—your posture, gait, facial expressions, and even your appearance—can send non-verbal messages and evoke different emotions from those you interact with. All of this happens before you utter a single word. You non-verbally communicate how others should perceive you and influence their feelings about you through your movements and appearance, all before you get a chance to amaze them with your talent.

There's no need to debate the merits of people's preferences and societal style choices. Fashion and trends are subject to change. The main point here is that we live in a visually oriented world. It's essential to be aware of and in control of this. This doesn't imply censoring yourself or catering to the tastes of others; it means being self-aware and understanding how you present yourself and what you desire. Be confident in presenting yourself as you see fit. Know that if you enter a room at 6 foot 3 with a cheetah mohawk, you'll elicit a particular response. Be ready to accept that and steer it toward your desired outcome. Prodigy performers exude confidence in being true to themselves.

Now, let's position ourselves for the optimal experience and the desired emotions at any given moment. Once again, this is a matter of choice and can be somewhat controlled. It's also one of the most beneficial things you can do for yourself. Prodigy performers don't leave this to chance; they've typically given it significant thought. How do you influence the room with your energy? Are you aware of your ability to shift the energy and mood in a room solely through your presence, not to mention your words and actions? Shaping the feelings you want rather than merely absorbing the emotions around you is one of the most valuable Prodigy Performance Habits to master. This is the simplest way to harmonize with others. Prodigy performers understand that it's up to them to determine how they direct the atmosphere in the room. Opinions aren't as crucial as your desired outcome. Assess the overall vibe in the room and guide it, focusing on the collective feeling rather than the individuals. Attempting to change people is futile. Instead, start populating your surroundings with people who intrigue you and contribute to the conversation.

Negative energy can be draining and all-consuming. Personal preferences are not the focus here. Prodigies observe what's happening and work toward a clean energy direction with a specific objective in mind. They can guide the room's atmosphere by separating their observations from evaluations and judgments. Opinions are irrelevant; what you want to happen is what matters. Prodigy performers are skilled at influencing the feeling in a room and often do it effortlessly. It becomes a part of who they are and something they're known for. People love being around them because they feel happier, less judged, and more confident in their presence.

You have the power to decide whether what you invest your time and energy in is worth it, both emotionally and physically. The empowerment in that choice is liberating. For a Prodigy Performer, the sense of wasted time is far worse than exhaustion. It's either hard work, or it's not worth doing. Why waste time on trivial, meaningless tasks when you have important, fulfilling goals to pursue? Wasting time holds you back from doing the things you love. Exploration, experimentation, and trial and error are valid and necessary as long as they lead to breakthroughs and growth. Ensure that you're enjoying the process and learning from it, or be prepared to pivot.

By always approaching challenges and hard work as choices rather than feeling forced into them, you will have a perspective that gives meaning to the work and makes it enjoyable. It removes the need for external recognition and provides a deeper personal satisfaction that leads to a more fulfilling journey. Prodigy Performers are less likely to get overwhelmed, communicate better, and generally have better relationships because they want to be where they are. When they enter a room, the energy is elevated. People are delighted to see Prodigies, and their presence is undeniable. Being around them, others feel more positive and uplifted.

As a dancer, it's easy to get lost in what's wrong with everything. Identifying flaws is a significant part of our training. However, the hard work doesn't seem so arduous, and the flaws don't appear as significant when you're doing it alongside a Prodigy because their mindset, motivation, and genuine emotions are evident. Those flaws become easier to address when that's your approach. How you feel and how you make others feel are choices. This can make a substantial difference not only for you but for everyone you interact with. Choose wisely.

ENERGY & ACTIONS

"There is nothing so useless as doing efficiently that which should not be done at all." -Peter Drucker.

As an ardent advocate of efficiency, the quote above carries significant weight. The crux of the matter lies in whether you are hoping, wishing, asking, or actively doing, being, and having. Your energy is not a fixed mental or physical state; it is a malleable entity that you shape through your thoughts, emotions, and the nourishment you provide to your body. Achieving success over the long haul is a demanding endeavor, and Prodigy Performers, as you might anticipate, excel in this domain due to their abundant reserves of energy, endurance, and motivation. They are proficient at maintaining unwavering mental focus throughout the day and possess the physical strength and stamina to outlast their peers because they refrain from squandering time on inconsequential pursuits.

Realizing this fact actually fuels them further. It's intrinsic to their identity and expectations of themselves. Success begets success, and the sensation of leading the pack provides a burst of happiness and fulfillment that replenishes the energy stores of Prodigy Performers.

If you aspire to achieve greater and more rapid results, channel additional energy into your endeavors, and you will witness a corresponding increase in your output. This bears significant importance, as energy is intricately connected to productivity. Disregard any preconceived limitations on what can be accomplished within a 24-hour day; posting about it on social media won't make it happen. Talk is cheap; you are capable of much more. Elevate your productivity in everything you do. Surpass all expectations. The average is never sufficient.

Do a little more; a lot of times

Let's conduct a test. Dedicate a little extra effort to everything you do for an entire day and see how it feels. Rise 15 minutes earlier with a clear intent to accomplish more. Add an extra set to your workout, and extend your time on the cardio machine by an extra 5 minutes. Now, envision doing this three, five, or ten times more frequently. Contemplate the surge in productivity, energy, and satisfaction that you will experience. Then, imagine inspiring others to do the same in order to advance towards your goals. Even a little bit multiplied by X adds up over time.

In finances, compound interest operates on the principle of exponential growth. Unlike simple interest, which is calculated only on the initial principal amount, compound interest considers both the principal and the accumulated interest. As interest accrues over time, the overall amount grows exponentially, resulting in a snowball effect that can substantially increase the total value of an investment. YOU are the investment! Do more, even if it's a little, and watch the interest compound!

Laser focus

While I appreciate having numerous options, too many choices can scatter your energy. Chart a clear course with a laser focus on what you aim to achieve. Focus concentrated attention on a singular objective, cutting through distractions and honing in on the task at hand with precision. Prodigy Performers have the ability to channel one's mental energy with unwavering intensity, excluding peripheral noise and maintaining a steadfast commitment to a specific goal. Like a focused laser, the mental clarity Prodigies develop enables individuals to dissect problems, navigate challenges, and execute tasks with unparalleled efficiency. Laser focus is not merely about looking at just one thing; it is about seeing through it, understanding its essence, and dedicating undivided attention to the pursuit of excellence. Those who exhibit laser focus often stand out as visionaries, problem solvers, and achievers who can illuminate paths to success with unmatched precision and determination. They are called Prodigy Performers!

Time is more limited than you realize, and you're likely not utilizing it as efficiently as you think. Maintain a log of how you spend your entire day. I bet you'll be astounded by the amount of time wasted on low-priority tasks. In essence, understanding the value of time is a catalyst for a purpose-driven existence; each day becomes an opportunity to create and achieve. Distill your focus on the most important task at hand and set your own rules for completing it. Do whatever it takes to make it an "I've got this" moment, and then follow through. You've got this, and the next task, and the one after that, and so on, for as long as you keep investing effort. Complete each task and banish excuses. It's done; move on!

Efficiency is imperative

Continually practicing something incorrectly remains incorrect, just as investing 100% effort and receiving a 70% return is an immense waste of your exertion. Efficiency is the art of accomplishing tasks with maximum output and minimal waste, a cornerstone principle in the pursuit of productivity and effectiveness. Prioritize finding the most direct route to your desired success and pursue it, ensuring that each action contributes meaningfully to the overarching goal. It's about eliminating unnecessary steps, honing in on key objectives, and leveraging tools and methodologies that enhance output without compromising quality. Don't settle for repeating the same incorrect outcome multiple times.

Identify the issue

Critical thinking is a vital component of the learning process. If you're not progressing despite genuine effort, then something is amiss. There is power in acknowledging and addressing this. It's time to recalibrate and dive back in. Prodigy Performers don't squander time or energy on pursuits misaligned with their plan. Identifying problems is a critical skill; all the actions in the world won't help unless you correctly identify the issue. Be explicit in recognizing what is amiss and why it's problematic so that you can rectify it. This realization is a valuable gift that will propel you further and faster than nearly anything else.

Do the math!

Physics is a fundamental principle. It's often said that the shortest path from point A to point B is a straight line, and if that's true, it's unchangeable. This is a critical point to remember when your path starts winding in various directions. Having too many options, answers, and opinions from so-called "experts" typically leads to undesirable outcomes. Stay focused, and remember that if you're unsatisfied, you can always try a different path. Experiment fully with one path, and if it doesn't work, try another. Keep trying until you're satisfied, but remember you can't change the math. Use a different formula if you want a different answer.

Get to it

If you find yourself procrastinating, it's likely an indicator that you don't have a genuine passion for what you're creating or contributing. Prodigy Performers simply don't postpone what they can do today. They don't leave tasks unfinished. It's time to reevaluate your desired outcome.

Want to get ahead but unsure how to accomplish everything you want within a day, week, month, or year? Prodigy Performers learn to create time. Yes, you heard that correctly. They can craft additional time through creative approaches, optimizing their activities to maximize efficiency. They make one task serve as a catalyst for another. Ensure that the activities you invest your time in are worthwhile. If the ratio of time invested to the rewards reaped is skewed, it's time to reconsider. Even if you don't mind a particular task, if it's no longer increasing your worth mentally, physically, or financially, delegate it to someone else. Learn to ask for help and determine where your time can be spent in a more valuable, productive manner. Engaging in mundane tasks solely because you can or always have is one of the primary reasons people run out of time or make excuses about time scarcity. You can't wash dishes indefinitely and hope to own the restaurant. Progress is essential, and the choice is yours. Prioritizing your time is crucial.

Prodigies always aim to make a remarkable impression. I used to favor the idea of underpromising and overdelivering, but now I believe in overpromising and overdelivering. Why should I understate my capabilities? Doing so would mean I know I'm exceptional but would need to pretend to be merely good. Essentially, I'd have to downplay my true potential to impress with what I knew I could accomplish all along. Where's the fun in that? Prodigy Performers understand that the pressure to impress is a potent motivator. They aim for greatness and either meet or raise the bar. Say what you do, then do what you say - with interest. This is a choice that many immensely talented individuals may not fully grasp. You can either rise and prepare to shine, or you can roll out of bed with the talent to do the job, sleep your way through it, and rinse and repeat until you're bored and disinterested. The impression you make on others varies significantly based on your desire to impress. Prodigy Performers lead by setting a compelling example.

People love to help. This can be challenging for Prodigies to adapt to because they often prefer doing everything themselves. It's a concept I still struggle to remember. Utilize the resources and people around you to free up time for what truly matters.

MASTERING TIME MANAGEMENT

Time management is a crucial skill for Prodigy Performers, and it goes beyond being punctual. Prodigies utilize their time wisely within a class or rehearsal. There's hardly a moment of rest during a Prodigy's dance class. Every extra second is dedicated to revisiting and perfecting the choreography, both physically and mentally, to ensure peak performance. Those additional minutes spent rehearsing while other groups are active accumulate over time. Those 15 minutes before class, dedicated to purposeful stretching and warming up, add up. More often than not, dancers you observe practicing vigorously on the sidelines while other groups perform are the Prodigy Performers, the elite dancers in the room. They mentally process information and leave nothing to chance, ensuring that they improve faster and perform better than their peers. It's a simple premise: if you use your time wisely, you'll achieve more.

Procrastination is a detrimental habit that can cascade into a series of equally undesirable behaviors. It typically starts with rationalizing the need to postpone tasks, followed by procrastination. The more you indulge in procrastination, the easier it becomes. This slippery slope can lead to a loss of focus and commitment.

The most effective shortcut is to learn from the mistakes of others and avoid making the same ones. Recognizing the challenges that others have faced and how they overcame them is essential for Prodigy's efficiency. Learn from the experiences of those who have gone before you. Prodigy Performers conduct extensive testing and rehearsal during practice, leaving no room for uncertainty in their performances. They've visualized their desired outcomes, developed muscle memory, and honed their skills to perfection.

Prodigies possess the remarkable ability to focus entirely on the task at hand and block out external distractions. This ability sets them apart from individuals with natural talent who lack the discipline to maintain it. It's ingrained in them and practiced to the point that it becomes second nature. Just as you don't consciously think about your next breath, Prodigy Performers don't need to think about focusing – they've mastered it.

The power of self-confidence and self-control is invigorating. This self-assuredness stems from practicing Prodigy Performance habits. They operate under the premise that "you don't rise to the occasion; you sink to your level of training." Train for greatness. Success begets more success. Build momentum by achieving your goals and setting even more ambitious ones. Turn yourself into a magnet for success by practicing for it and making it a habit. The results you achieve are a direct reflection of your practice. Strive to reach a level of undeniable excellence.

KEEPING THE BALL ROLLING

Many individuals wait until they face significant problems before making changes or seeking assistance with their issues. It doesn't have to be this way. Prodigy Performers have cultivated the habit of going beyond their capabilities when things are going exceptionally well. Why wait until you're in a hole before deciding to climb out of it? Instead, embrace the habit of self-improvement during moments of positivity. This is where the true magic lies. Learning is a continuous process available to you, and it's most effectively absorbed when you're not grappling with other negative issues.

Perhaps you've observed other dancers advancing more rapidly than you. They seem to bypass the steps that took you ages to master. Do you know a dancer who consistently wins scholarships or secures the spot you desire? Do they always appear to be in the right place at the right time? Even when they stumble, do they maintain a remarkable presence and are adored by all? What's their secret? How can you tap into that?

My hypothesis is that they are Prodigy Performers and their secret lies in their habits! The good news is with effort and persistence, you can join their ranks. Regardless of your current situation, background, personality, weaknesses, or excuses, it doesn't matter. If you're on the right path and frustrated by slow progress, it's time to reconsider your approach. Study those who are achieving what you aspire to do and integrate these Prodigy Performance habits into your life. This will be a game-changer and precisely what you need to attain and maintain Prodigy status.

"Obsession is a word the lazy use to describe the dedicated." — Unknown.

Talent alone is insufficient. Your life should be filled with healthy obsessions—meaning things you are passionate about, whether you're excellent at them or still learning. Yes, I mentioned "healthy obsessions." Society tends to stigmatize obsession as a negative concept, advocating balance and baby steps. I disagree. Why would I invest my heart in something I'm not obsessed with? Why settle for baby steps that will never position me to realize my ambitions? If you have grand dreams, and I bet you do, you must be obsessed with your hopes and aspirations and channel all your energy into them, or they have little chance of materializing. Moreover, for Prodigy Performers, these obsessions contribute to a balanced and well-rounded life, nurturing both their mental and physical well-being. Extraordinary achievements cannot be realized with average effort. Choose obsessions that bring joy, serve a positive purpose, and are in harmony with your well-being. Obsess over everything you love and continually seek new passions and obsessions. By channeling energy into endeavors that align with your values and aspirations, healthy obsessions become a positive force that enriches the journey of personal development and contributes to a fulfilling and purposeful life.

HIT THE REBOOT BUTTON

Don't be afraid to reboot. For Prodigy Performers, this can be challenging, given their intense focus and determination in everything they do. However, a reboot can inject new energy, clear your mind, and elevate your overall happiness. Happy individuals tend to create and enjoy a more fulfilling life. It's crucial to be genuinely interested in what you're working on; nobody desires to consistently struggle with an unfulfilling task. Remember, you have complete control over this. Setting intentions for your energy is a valuable practice for Prodigy Performers. Before engaging in an activity, ask yourself, "What energy do I need to bring to this to achieve the desired feeling?" This question helps you assess whether the activity is worth your energy and what level of intensity it requires for a Prodigy Performance. Understanding your time and energy allocation for a project can prevent you from wasting hours on unimportant tasks that don't serve your overarching goals.

Taking a break, whether it's a short pause during work or an extended vacation, offers a range of advantages for mental, physical, and emotional well-being.

Stress Reduction:

Breaks provide a crucial opportunity to step away from the demands of work and responsibilities, allowing the mind to decompress. Whether it's a brief walk, a few moments of deep breathing, or a more extended vacation, taking a break helps reduce stress levels, promoting better overall mental health.

Enhanced Productivity:

Paradoxically, taking breaks can lead to increased productivity. Regular breaks prevent burnout, boost focus, and refresh cognitive abilities. They provide a chance for the brain to recharge, which can result in improved concentration and efficiency when returning to tasks.

Improved Creativity and Problem-Solving:

Stepping away from a problem or a challenging task allows the brain to process information subconsciously. This downtime often sparks creative insights and facilitates problem-solving. Breaks provide the mental space for new perspectives and ideas to emerge.

Enhanced Mood and Well-being:

Taking breaks has a positive impact on mood and emotional well-being. Engaging in activities one enjoys during a break, whether it's reading, listening to music, or spending time outdoors, contributes to a more positive mindset and reduces feelings of monotony or burnout. Whether it's practicing mindfulness, taking a nap, or enjoying a hobby, these moments of self-care contribute to better mental and emotional balance, fostering a sense of fulfillment and happiness.

Stronger Relationships:

Extended breaks, such as vacations, provide an opportunity to connect with family and friends, strengthening social bonds. Quality time spent with loved ones fosters a sense of belonging, support, and overall emotional resilience.

Taking breaks is not just a luxury but a strategic investment in overall well-being and performance. Whether short respites throughout the day or longer vacations, breaks contribute to a healthier and more balanced life, enhancing physical health, mental resilience, and overall satisfaction.

Avoid energy traps

Showing up is merely the first step for Prodigy Performers. They avoid energy traps – situations and people that deplete more energy than they provide. Those who give mediocre attention to tasks will inevitably experience diminishing results, potentially leading to their eventual failure. Engaging in activities that replenish your energy while investing your efforts allows you to produce more and maintain balance and well-being. Prioritizing creation, quality, and output frequency is vital for long-term career success. This doesn't mean you need to be miserly with your time and energy but rather ensure you allocate time to recharge and find continued inspiration.

The concept of necessity is paramount.

Prodigy Performers understand that greatness is not a mandate; it's a personal commitment. You don't have to be great at anything – you must want to be great. You can coast through life using your natural talents, but that's not the path to a successful and fulfilling dance career. Prodigy Performers deliberately raise their level of necessity. Everything is a choice, including the choice to be extraordinary. It's a matter of whether you want it or demand it for yourself. These habits are not for those content with mediocrity; they require unwavering commitment and a rejection of luck and chance. Tenacity is often more crucial than talent.

Success is the only option

Prodigy Performers accomplish their goals because they have no alternative. They strive for greatness because they couldn't live with themselves otherwise – their standards are exceptionally high. They operate with an innate sense of destiny, an unshakeable belief that success is the only option. Their drive makes them accountable at a higher level than their peers.

Acceptable outcomes demand a Prodigy Performance every time. It's an obligation, a personal duty, tied to their identity. This relentless drive separates Prodigies from the rest, and personal standards of excellence are a powerful force in long-term success. Prodigy Performers set the bar higher, care about details, and, most importantly, finish what they start. They understand that obsession is not a negative word; it's a description of their capacity to give more, work harder, and never give up.

When does this obsession end? When you follow through and finish every task, no matter how small. Celebrating these successes and moving the finish line forward recharges energy and confidence, keeping Prodigy Performers believing in their extraordinariness. They expect themselves to make things happen, and they do. Then, it's on to the next obsession. This journey is stimulating, challenging, and personally satisfying. Prodigy Performers thrive on internal pressure, although this might not be normal for most people. The sense of duty and obligation to a higher vision, mission, or calling drives them through hardships and pushes them to succeed out of necessity. Then, as long as the passion remains, they move to the finish line and keep working.

Make it look good

In the realm of dance, I have a fundamental mantra: A dancer's job is to "Make it look good." Whether you adore the style and choreography or not, Prodigy Performers always strive to make every movement look flawless. This was a concept I didn't fully grasp as a young dancer. I once believed that I had to like a piece of choreography before I could make it look good. Regrettably, this way of thinking undoubtedly caused me to miss out on numerous opportunities and auditions. Had I adhered to the simple standard of doing my job and "making it look good," regardless of personal preference, I would have booked more and had a much more fulfilling journey. Instead, I allowed myself to get caught up in my ego, my personal preferences, my self-image, and if I looked and felt cool. I wanted the comfort and enjoyment of a specific style, losing sight of my primary responsibility as a dancer. To make it look good!

PRACTICE MAKES PERFECT

Your practice defines your performance, and it reflects who you are. Much like the saying, "You get what you pay for," you will undoubtedly receive precisely what you practice for. The dance journey often involves enduring self-inflicted hardship, a willingness to potentially repeat a sequence thousands of times until it's perfected. This endurance is what distinguishes the greats. To become a Prodigy Performer, you must possess the inner drive and discipline of a professional athlete combined with the artistry and grace of a painter. Obsession isn't a disease; it's a gift that fuels relentless pursuit. Those who claim otherwise likely have never operated at the highest level. You manifest the results of your thoughts, and if your obsessive pursuit of your dreams brings you happiness, that obsession is not only healthy but also entirely valid.

Prodigies are experts at pushing their limits while preserving their physical well-being. They've mastered the art of training to perform without injuries and can effectively recognize and address minor issues before they escalate into chronic injuries. This is particularly challenging for dancers with high pain tolerance, who often push through discomfort. Your body is your instrument; it's invaluable and should be treated accordingly. To ensure a lengthy dance career, knowing and taking care of your body is paramount. It's ok to push your boundaries but know your limits and respect your body.

Arrive at your dance rehearsals and performances with the confidence of someone who belongs there. If you don't always enjoy rehearsal, that's alright – focus on getting it right quickly and moving forward. Some professionals relish the experience of taking classes and rehearsing, while others have opted not to take a class in years, preferring minimal rehearsals. Once you reach this level, there's no definitive right or wrong approach. The key is to understand who you are and what you need, communicate your preferences clearly, and do your job, "Always make it look good."

Say it out loud

Prodigies are proficient at articulating their goals to themselves and others and working efficiently toward them. Verbalizing your objectives, both during practice and when communicating with teachers, mentors, family, and friends, holds you accountable. Once you verbalize your intentions, you create a commitment to fulfill them. This public commitment, backed by integrity, propels you to new heights. The effective practice also involves knowing what questions to ask – not just happening upon the answers. It's about striking a balance, knowing when to step back, evaluating your situation, posing questions, and making necessary adjustments. Remember that everything is interconnected, and beating yourself up in the name of practice or obsession is counterproductive. Maintain control, be calculated, apply the principles of physics, and do the math. Pushing through physical barriers is essential, but brute force is unsustainable and usually not the long-term answer.

RISKING IT ALL: MAKING MISTAKES

"You miss 100% of the shots you don't take." - *Wayne Gretzky.*

What do you fear deep down but are reluctant to admit? Is it the fear of failure? The dread of people disliking you or what you present? Risk is an essential element on your path to reaping rewards. To achieve greatness, you must be willing to risk the possibility of others disapproving of you or your work. Besides, the realm of the everyday, universally accepted concepts, ideas, and methods has already been thoroughly explored, often leading to mediocrity, monotony, and carbon copies. Whenever doubt creeps in, ask yourself this: "What is the worst thing that could happen?" If the answer doesn't involve severe harm or death to yourself or others, then you're on the right track. Fear, when harnessed correctly, heightens your senses, making you feel alive and more focused. It ushers you into a state of heightened excitement and awareness, preparing your mind and body for the impending challenges. Rather than battling fear, befriend it and challenge it to a dance-off!

Some people make it their life's mission to avoid risk at all costs, but Prodigy Performers embrace it. Risk is, in fact, one of the most vital ingredients in the recipe for success. Uncertainty is where we learn and grow. Placing yourself in new and uncharted territory compels creativity and pushes your limits. The sense of risk assigns worth to your endeavors and acts as an indicator of whether you're striving hard enough. You must be prepared to invest your time, energy, and financial resources into your obsessions. Sometimes, you will lose them. Ever heard of the line "If it was easy, everyone would be doing it"? Exactly.

"If you set your goals ridiculously high and it's a failure, you will fail above everyone else's success." -James Cameron.

You might not view this as a significant risk because it's an integral part of who you are and what you do, but many others will. This may include those you love most. Taking risks can attract critics and naysayers, but it's a part of the adventure. If you harbor grand, audacious goals and you're pushing boundaries, the prospect of numerous risks should be exhilarating. Challenge yourself by pondering, "What do I stand to lose?" Then, make the decision that aligns with your life's current circumstances. Yes, you risk not succeeding and depleting your resources of time, energy, and money. But remember, without risk, there is no reward. You can generate more energy and money, but the only resource you'll eventually run out of is time. Don't squander it. Prodigy Performers possess the belief that they make sound decisions and invest an appropriate level of risk in each situation. Risk inevitably comes with the potential for failure, but that's precisely what makes it a challenge.

I recall reading that it takes around 12 years to become a doctor, followed by additional years to establish a practice. In our fast-paced world, people often measure success in significantly shorter timeframes. When you think that something is taking too long, remember that most professions require 8 to 10 years to attain a minimal level of competence. It's only deemed a complete failure when you quit. If you need more time, take it.

"Everyone has a plan 'till they get punched in the mouth." -Mike Tyson.

If you aren't making initial mistakes, chances are you're not tackling difficult enough challenges. If you're repeatedly making simple mistakes, you are the problem. Differentiate between these types of errors and adapt accordingly. Paying close attention to details is crucial because many failures are the culmination of uncorrected minor mistakes along the way. Identifying and rectifying these minor mistakes early can prevent major failures.

I WANNA BE LIKE YOU!

"You will get all you want in life if you help enough other people get what they want." -Zig Ziglar.

Your gift to the world is simply being yourself. Leading by example is an intrinsic part of a Prodigy Performer's journey. It's a cliché, but it holds the truth. You must help yourself before you can help others. When leaders consistently model the values, work ethic, and principles they advocate, it fosters a sense of credibility and authenticity. People are more likely to trust and respect a leader who practices what they preach.

By prioritizing self-development and success, Prodigies are equipped to make a broader and more profound impact on the lives of those around them. They are catalysts for transformative, positive change. Others strive to emulate them as they set the bar high, not just in terms of physical talent but also in their character, embodying kindness, honesty, and unwavering hard work. Prodigies can influence others to enhance their own characters, leading to growth for all involved. Elevating those around you not only benefits them but also inspires you to aim higher.

Actions often speak louder than words. This alignment of words and deeds promotes a shared sense of purpose, fosters a collaborative environment, and establishes a positive work ethic. When Prodigies exhibit resilience, adaptability, and a strong work ethic, it encourages others to adopt similar attitudes. This, in turn, contributes to increased productivity and a more engaged and motivated event. The benefits of leading by example extend far beyond the individual leader, positively influencing the entire team and organizational culture of everything they are a part of. By embodying the values and behaviors they wish to instill, Prodigies become not only guides but also sources of inspiration, fostering an environment conducive to success, collaboration, and personal and professional development.

"I am my own experiment. I am my own work of art." – Madonna.

Have you ever met someone you instantly liked? Despite knowing nothing about them, there's something about their aura that radiates positivity, making you feel good in their presence. This energy and enthusiasm, a hallmark of Prodigy Performance habits, have the power to uplift and make people feel better merely by their presence.

Prodigies derive immense satisfaction from being role models, often taking up roles as mentors, teachers, and influencers. They grasp the bigger picture of how they can contribute to a group's transformation. The introduction of a Prodigy Performer into any team doesn't only elevate the performance of the team due to their exceptional talent but often spurs everyone in the group to work harder and aim for greatness. People tend to match the example set for them and yearn to live up to the expectations. Standards rise all around, fostering growth.

Sharing the path they've walked and currently enjoy with others brings Prodigies a sense of accomplishment. With their focus on continuous learning and developing all dance-related skills, recognition, and financial rewards are natural outcomes of the excellence they attain. Success and contentment are inevitable. These positive feelings guide Prodigy Performers on their continual quest to feel good and enjoy life. It may get lonely at the top, but boosting others gives them a renewed sense of purpose and allows them to do more, have more, and be more.

Assisting and inspiring others not only feels good but also earns respect. Respect, however, is earned and is a reflection of one's character. Prodigy Performance habits instill the knowledge that respect is being granted. This realization serves as another guiding principle, keeping them on their chosen path. Many of these habits don't require you to seek external validation because the reward is already built in. As you seamlessly practice these habits, a natural symbiotic exchange unfolds. External accolades become the icing on the cake. You'll witness others emulating your actions and influenced by your behavior, perhaps even witnessing copycats. Don't be alarmed; in this context, imitation is indeed the sincerest form of flattery. It's a Prodigy Performer's duty to inspire the next generation, making them aspire to be like you.

ENJOY THE JOURNEY

"Often when you think you are at the end of something, you're at the beginning of something else." -Fred Rogers, creator of Mister Rogers' Neighborhood.

Why invest years of hard work in building a life and career and then never truly enjoy it? Prodigy Performers know when to pause and savor the moment. They are self-assured enough to recognize when they're doing great and commend themselves for a job well done. They hold themselves to exceptionally high standards, often the toughest critics to please. The fulfillment of loving what you do and excelling at it is what you're striving for.

Prodigies are continually adjusting their goals, so it can be challenging to identify when they've achieved certain milestones, both for themselves and others. The finish line is ever-moving. So when does it end? In truth, it doesn't. It ends when you do. Recognizing and acknowledging the small wins and milestones achieved along the way is crucial. It fosters positivity for everyone involved and serves as a reminder that everyone is one step closer to realizing another dream.

Embracing the process is essential and a reminder of your own greatness. Take a look at everything you have accomplished and are currently doing. You've made all of this happen! How incredible are you? It begins with your recognition of this fact. If you don't believe it, who else will? You are amazing, and you are continuously shaping your life according to your design. Remember, you have complete control over your happiness through your thoughts and habits.

With that said, enjoying success is different from resting on past accomplishments. Prodigy Performers don't get bogged down in the past because they are always striving for new levels of greatness. Although the process and work are fulfilling, they don't get caught up gazing out the window or in the rearview mirror. Focusing on the destination is the primary aim. Then, it's on to the next adventure. While each new endeavor ignites the creative process, delivering immense joy, the completion of each task is equally satisfying.

SECTION 8: OUTSIDE INFLUENCES / WHO'S YOUR CREW

"Keep away from those who try to belittle your ambitions. Small people always do that, but the really great make you believe that you too can become great."

-Mark Twain.

SURROUND YOURSELF WITH THE RIGHT PEOPLE

I firmly believe that "like energies attract." It's vital to be aware of how this principle is influencing your life. One of the surefire ways to undo years of hard work is by surrounding yourself with the wrong people. Recognize that your surroundings and the company you keep can significantly influence your goals and aspirations. It's time to intentionally surround yourself with the best, most positive, and inspiring individuals you can find. This realization has been the linchpin of my success. Your inner circle should consist of those who share your aspirations and engage in pursuits similar to yours. People tend to reveal their core attributes rather swiftly. Failing to recognize who people are at their core and their true impact on your life can be detrimental.

Make your choices based on the quality of the people you'll be collaborating with. This doesn't necessarily mean they all have to be dancers, but they should vibrate on a high, positive frequency. Surround yourself with individuals who inspire you, and expect exceptional efforts from everyone. Align yourself with supporters who cheer you on without conditions. Your social environment has a profound impact on your ability to attain and sustain Prodigy Performance levels.

Researchers have discovered that bad behaviors tend to proliferate within certain social clusters, just as positive behaviors thrive in similar environments. It may sometimes be challenging to select your social circle, particularly at a young age. Factors like your location, financial situation, and family life play a significant role in the options available to you. Negotiating certain groups within a studio or industry can be tricky. Nevertheless, Prodigy Performers must strive to avoid negative influences and social dysfunction. Keep your long-term goals in mind. Be strategic and consistent in selecting the individuals you spend time with and those who hold influencing power over you. Your social circle is a choice and a direct reflection of your character. Don't hesitate to move on when necessary. Growth happens at different paces for everyone. You're setting your goals for yourself, not others. The more success you achieve, the more quickly those without a similar trajectory may try to undermine and impede your progress. Let these people go.

"You are the average of the five people you spend the most time with." - Jim Rohn.

Bid farewell to negativity. Even more damaging than overt haters are the naysayers. Remember, these can be friends and, often, even family members and teachers. They love you and supposedly wish the best for you. The issue is that they might never comprehend that fulfilling your obsessions is genuinely what's best for you, possibly because they've never done it themselves. They will perpetually attempt to dissuade you from the necessary path to greatness and steer you toward a safe, average choice. They will always possess negative examples of why you should avoid taking bold steps and aiming for excellence. Remember, you aren't aiming for average, and you'll never be content with holding yourself back. It's okay to be a bit selfish and audacious when your future is at stake. Let these individuals know that you appreciate their support but have no time for "what ifs." Average isn't an option for you; you're striving for more in every aspect of your life, including your dance career. You'll pursue more, become more, and have more, whether or not they cheer you on.

Seek mentorship from individuals who've accomplished significant and bold achievements. Connect with people you admire within the dance world and beyond. Put yourself in the right place at the right time and approach the right people. Finding the courage to reach out to a mentor you respect can be daunting, but most people respond to passion and a clear reason for your outreach.

Mentors should possess knowledge and experience in areas closely tied to your goals and have a genuine concern for your journey. Know the difference between a mentor and someone teaching a class. Recently, I have noticed an uptick in people who advertise themselves as mentors and charge crazy fees. It could be semantics, but I personally feel they are leveraging this generation's search for help for personal gain. That is not the definition of what I would call a true mentor.

Mentoring someone and teaching them in a class are distinctly different approaches to imparting knowledge and guidance, each with its own set of characteristics and objectives. Make sure you know the difference and put yourself in the appropriate relationship.

Nature of Relationship:

• **Mentoring:** Mentoring typically involves a more personalized, one-on-one relationship. The mentor serves as a guide, offering support, advice, and sharing personal experiences to help the mentee develop both professionally and personally.

• **Teaching in a Class:** Teaching in a class usually involves a group setting where a teacher imparts knowledge to multiple students. The relationship is often more formal, with a focus on delivering structured content to a larger audience.

Focus and Scope:

• **Mentoring:** The focus of mentoring extends beyond academic or technical knowledge. It often encompasses broader aspects of personal development, career growth, and the cultivation of soft skills.

• **Teaching in a Class:** Teaching in a class typically concentrates on delivering a specific curriculum, covering a set of topics or subjects within a defined scope.

Individualization:

• **Mentoring:** Mentoring allows for a more personalized and flexible approach. The mentor can tailor advice and guidance to the unique needs, goals, and learning styles of the mentee.

• **Teaching in a Class:** Teaching in a class often follows a more standardized approach, with a fixed curriculum and set teaching methods designed to accommodate a diverse group of students.

Long-term vs. Short-term:

- **Mentoring:** Mentoring relationships often develop over an extended period, fostering a long-term connection. Mentors provide ongoing support and guidance as the mentee progresses in their personal and professional journey.

- **Teaching in a Class:** Teaching in a class is often more short-term and course-oriented. The teacher imparts knowledge within the duration of a specific class or semester, with less emphasis on a sustained, individualized relationship.

While having a variety of mentors is beneficial, be cautious not to overwhelm yourself with too many conflicting opinions. Choose your mentors wisely and keep them close. Maintain regular check-ins with them, whether it's weekly or monthly. These check-ins will help them guide you and hold you accountable as you progress on your path. Pose questions, be a good listener, but always make your own decisions. It's your life to lead, and your decisions will allow you to take full responsibility while leaving no room for excuses. The best shortcut to success is to learn from those who've traveled the path before you, avoiding the mistakes that saved their time, finances, and energy.

Select teachers and mentors who bring joy and growth into your life, whether you're in the spotlight or facing challenges. When people care, they go the extra mile to understand you and offer help when needed. Align yourself with individuals who can position you in the right places. Build relationships based on trust and loyalty, and they will endure. Forge mutually beneficial friendships that leverage your strengths and those of your counterparts. Use one another as reminders of your shared goals and help each other develop your respective areas.

Once you adopt this approach, opportunities that may take others years to access will suddenly become available to you. This is your time to shine and demonstrate your Prodigy Performance habits, which will lead to even more opportunities.

PARENTS AND SUPPORT SYSTEMS

"Parents can only give good advice or put them on the right paths, but the final forming of a person's character lies in their own hands." - Anne Frank.

To me, this is perhaps the most uniquely influential and vital section of all. We could elaborate and scrutinize every angle, but I prefer to keep it concise. A dancer's early support system can play a significant role in their initiation and provide ongoing structure. Everyone comes from various backgrounds, which include geographical, emotional, financial, and cultural factors. However, this doesn't determine the success of Prodigy Performers. In fact, both sides of this coin can serve as strong motivation. It's all about perspective – some dancers have excellent family and studio support, some fall in the middle, and some have none. Many have been taught by exceptional teachers from a young age, while others are relatively new to the dance world or haven't had the privilege of learning from great teachers. You have what you have, and it's not a deal-breaker either way. Recognizing all aspects and addressing what's needed is crucial.

There are many incredibly successful dancers with support systems at both ends of the spectrum. For every Prodigy Performer with strong family and studio support, good habits, and economic advantages, there are just as many, if not more, who had none of that and yet have achieved great success. They've often used the absence of these advantages as fuel for their ambition.

For every overbearing "Dance Mom" who might exert too much pressure, there's an absentee parent who can't provide enough attention. For every supportive teacher challenging and nurturing their students, there's a mean and dismissive one failing to do either. Both sides of the coin are in play here. Avoid dwelling on excuses or self-pity. Each situation is unique, and the key is to acknowledge yours and determine your plan of action. The blame game won't help you; look to your future and make a plan.

The good news is, as stated in a great quote: "Your present circumstances don't determine where you go; they merely determine where you start." Realize that friends and family should support your growth, not hinder it. It can be challenging to accept when this isn't happening, but there are many people in the world willing to offer support, both emotionally and even financially. You can find the support you need, but you may need to search for it. Establish open lines of communication with everyone around you, let them know your needs, and you will find the support. Don't be afraid to ask for or accept help. Ensure that those you're drawn to possess the qualities you're ready to nurture. When people know what you want and need, it's much easier for them to offer support in helping you reach your dreams. Don't settle for "Someone told me that, and I believed them." Make your own decisions; it's your life to live. You are in control of who and what influences you.

KNOW YOUR TEACHERS

"It is the supreme art of the teacher to awaken joy in creative expression and knowledge." - Albert Einstein.

Teachers play a pivotal role in the development of dancers. Some are fortunate to learn from dedicated educators who impart not just style and technique but also valuable life qualities. However, some may not have had this privilege. If you find yourself somewhere in the middle, it's time for a change. Getting to know your teachers is essential.

Prodigy Performers actively seek out the best teachers and mentors in the industry. Factors like time, money, geography, and age may seem like barriers, but they're only temporary if you're determined and willing to put in the effort. Prodigies define their wants and needs and create a plan to achieve them.

Ask yourself: What are your goals, plans, dreams, and who can help you reach them? Clarity is crucial for efficiency. Are you truly learning from your teachers, or are you coasting on your talents? If you're just playing follow the leader in class, it's time to demand more, both from yourself and your teacher. Open up about your desires; you might be surprised by the impact of voicing your aspirations. It holds you accountable and prompts your teacher to be more attentive. It can also lead to more in-depth discussions that reshape their vision of you. Help them help you.

Understand what your teachers need from you to unlock the next level. Prodigy Performers precisely understand what they aim to learn from each instructor. It's time for some research and an honest conversation with your director to ensure you're on the same page. Why are you attending their class? Is it mandatory social, or have you always done it? Does it lead to mentorship, assisting, or potential work? And most importantly, is it working? You should have the answers to these questions, and your teachers should know what you're actively seeking from them. Revisit these questions regularly, like an open-book test. When you know what information you're looking for, finding the answers becomes much easier.

Apart from your current school or studio, who else are you training with? Take advantage of online options, conventions, and summer programs. This is a significant part of your goal-setting and planning. Choose wisely to match your wants and needs. Seek teachers who inspire you and provide different perspectives.

It should be every studio and teacher's goal to pour their knowledge and preparation into you, enabling you to surpass and transcend them. While this can be challenging for some, it's an essential realization. It doesn't mean you discard them; Prodigy Performers are grateful and know when to give credit. It means that there's a time for every bird to fly. Ensuring everyone is aligned with your goals can prevent hard feelings. Communication is key.

STUDIOS AND DANCE PROGRAMS

Where you train and the programs you're involved in can make a significant difference. An excellent teacher who aligns with your goals is invaluable. If you've been training at the same studio since childhood, ask yourself annually if the studio continues to develop you or if it's already taught you everything it can. It's a tough question for everyone involved but an important one.

Outgrowing your studio doesn't negate the incredible training and foundation they've provided. This is likely the place that ignited your passion for dance and built your strong technical base. Many times, the answer isn't to move on but to supplement your training with additional opportunities. Take the time to research, visit, and assess programs based on finding the best fit for your needs and goals.

Here are key factors to consider when looking for traditional and additional dance studios, convention events, and programs:

Qualified and Experienced Instructors:

• Ensure the instructors are accessible, experienced, qualified, and well-trained teachers.

• Look for instructors who are passionate about dance and committed to their students' growth. They are not just looking to supplement performing income by standing in front of a class, videoing themselves dancing, and taking photos at the end.

Wide Range of Classes:

• A good studio/program should offer a variety of dance styles and levels to cater to different interests and skill levels.

• Check the class rates and schedule to ensure it fits with your availability and is worth it.

Positive Learning Environment:

• The studio/event should have a supportive and encouraging atmosphere.

• Look for a place that fosters creativity, teamwork, and positive reinforcement.

Clean and Safe Facilities:

• Ensure the studio/venue is clean, well-maintained, and equipped with proper dance floors to prevent injuries.

• Check for safety measures, especially if it's for a child, such as secure entrances and exits.

Student Opportunities:

• Look for studios/events that provide performance opportunities, competitions, or showcases to allow students to apply what they've learned.

Community and Culture:

• A strong sense of community and a positive studio/event culture are crucial.

• Try to get a feel for the program by talking to existing students.

Reasonable Class Sizes:

• Manageable class sizes that ensure as much individualized attention as possible and better learning outcomes.

- Ensure the studio/event has room to dance.

Professionalism:

- The staff and instructors should be professional, organized, and communicate effectively.

- Look for studios/events with clear policies and guidelines.

Reputation:

- Research the studio/event's reputation by asking for opinions and recommendations from other dancers, studio directors & parents.

It's not advisable for dancers to leave the studio setting too early, hopping around as independents, substituting training for taking random convention classes. In fact, I advise against it. Structure in a good dance program at a young age is vital for consistent training and social development. However, failing to acknowledge that there may be more out there can lead to disinterest and plateauing. Prodigy Performers should and will get frustrated when this happens. Spinning your wheels out of loyalty, respect, ignorance, or fear of hurting feelings is unacceptable. A studio that truly cares about your development will understand this. In my opinion, they should be helping you discover all available opportunities. A studio should take pride in providing avenues for growth and development, including advanced classes, workshops, and/or guest instructors. Your future is about you, and different rules apply to everyone. Be the exception. It's time to learn more, be more, do more.

Prodigy Performers thrive in environments that prepare them for a dance career, not just for competitions or recitals. This means dance studios must continually learn and grow, staying current with industry changes in this digital age. Be clear with your studio about your expectations and intentions. Your teachers and studio directors must know your plans to effectively support you. Never settle for being "just one of the dancers" on the team. It's about you and your future, and it's time to have these conversations with your parents and dance teachers. Put a plan in place. Communication is key. Make choices that align with your desired path, studying under teachers and programs that will help you succeed. The essential ingredient is you.

THE SOCIAL DILEMMA

'How do we consume as much of your time and conscious attention as possible?'" — Sean Parker, the founding president of Facebook.

The initial thought process that went into building social media applications, Facebook (owner of Instagram) being the first of them. This quote underscores the intentional design of social media platforms to capture and hold user attention for extended periods, which can lead to addictive behaviors and a significant impact on mental health and well-being. It highlights the need for users to be mindful of their social media consumption and to actively manage their screen time to mitigate potential negative effects.

In today's world, more than ever, everything is interconnected. Dancers are building their personal brands from a very young age. Thanks to social media, mistakes are no longer private; they occur publicly. This includes training and development, which used to be a more private process, allowing for a broader range of positive and negative growth. No one witnessed the struggles. Now, training and development are part of the public display, and sometimes they are even fabricated. As with many people, I see both the positive and negative aspects of this social media reality show that is now considered daily life. There are many traps to be avoided, but also several exciting new opportunities to explore on various platforms.

As I mentioned earlier, the role of social media on dancers and society as a whole could fill an entire book, but I'll briefly touch on it again here. I believe there are two ways people approach social media: either resist it or embrace it. Those who advocate quitting social media entirely and putting their devices down are stuck in the past. Apologies, folks, but platforms like YouTube, Instagram, Facebook, Snapchat, TikTok, and whatever new platform emerges by the time I finish writing this are here to stay. We must embrace these platforms while being cautious not to become absorbed by them. Utilize each platform to your advantage for information and promotion, but remain authentic to yourself and your goals. Think of them as resources rather than places to reside or sources of validation. Each can offer something valuable, and when used properly, they can even lead to significant financial gain. However, the biggest challenge most people face with social media is time management. Make sure you're getting a return on your time investment, and remember that what you post is out there forever. Be smart about it.

Responsible use of social media is crucial in maintaining a healthy digital life and safeguarding your personal information. Here are some tips to help guide your social media use:

Think Before You Share

• **Privacy:** Consider the privacy implications of what you're sharing. Could it potentially harm you or someone else if seen by the wrong person?

• **Permanent:** Remember that what you post online can be permanent and might be seen by future employers, family, or friends.

Protect Your Personal Information

• **Security Settings:** Use the privacy settings on each platform to control who can see your information and posts.

• **Avoid Sharing Sensitive Info**: Refrain from sharing sensitive personal information like your address, phone number, or financial details.

Be Respectful and Kind

• **Avoid Negative Interactions:** Don't engage in cyberbullying or harassment. If you wouldn't say something in person, don't say it online.

• **Positive Communication:** Strive for positive and constructive communication.

• **Check Sources:** Make sure information is from a reliable source before sharing it.

• **Combat Misinformation:** Don't contribute to the spread of fake news or misinformation.

• **Consider Others' Perspectives:** Remember that people come from diverse backgrounds and may have different perspectives.

• **Avoid Jumping to Conclusions:** Don't make assumptions about people based on limited information.

Manage Your Time

• **Set Time Limits:** Consider setting limits on how much time you spend on social media each day.

• **Take Breaks:** Regularly take breaks from social media to disconnect and focus on other aspects of life.

• **Notice Impact on Mood:** Pay attention to how social media use impacts your mood and mental well-being, and adjust your usage accordingly.

Be Mindful of Your Digital Footprint

• **Future Impact:** Be aware that your digital footprint can have long-term implications.

• **Regular Clean-Up:** Periodically review your past posts and delete any that no longer reflect your views or could be seen as inappropriate.

Report and Block When Necessary

• **Report Abuse:** If you witness bullying, harassment, or other abusive behavior, report it to the platform.

• **Use Blocking Features:** Don't hesitate to block users who are harassing or causing distress.

Cultivate a Positive Online Community

• **Engage with Positive Content:** Follow accounts that inspire and uplift you.

• **Contribute Positively:** Share content that contributes positively to the online community.

• **Avoid Comparisons:** Social media often highlights the best moments of people's lives, leading to unrealistic comparisons. Focus on your own journey.

- **True to Yourself:** Stay true to yourself and avoid creating a false persona online.

Educate Yourself on Platform Policies

- **Understand User Agreements:** Be aware of the terms of service and community guidelines of the platforms you use.

- **Seek Support if Needed:** If social media use is negatively impacting your mental health, consider seeking support from friends, family, or a professional.

Practicing responsible social media use helps in creating a safer and more positive digital environment for yourself and others. It contributes to your personal well-being while also fostering a supportive online community. Be smart, be safe!

SECTION 9: HARD TRUTHS

"Most likely, the problem won't be around in a year, but my reputation of how I dealt with it will." - Whitney Cummings.

Are you ready for some hard truths? Can you handle them? Well, here's the unvarnished reality: nobody knows your limits, what you can or cannot achieve. What works for one person can be a total and complete failure for another. Anyone who says otherwise is not speaking the truth. Your path is uniquely yours. What consistently makes the difference is your mindset and your habits. Challenge anyone who says, "You can't." Ask them, "In whose world?" In your world, you can achieve almost anything you can think of. When you're fully present in your world, you decide what's possible. You determine what's sufficient and what needs more attention. You direct your thoughts and actions.

YOU ARE THE ULTIMATE DECISION-MAKER

By creating a world where you are the ultimate decision-maker, you wield great power. Some people find this power overwhelming because it leaves no room for excuses. If you fail to execute your plan, you have no one to blame but yourself. Nobody is forcing you to do anything. In the end, you have two choices: do something and be happy or not do it and be happy. Both are decisions and can lead to positive outcomes if managed properly. The key lies in your choice and your alignment with your desired direction. Anything beyond your control remains just that – beyond your control. Prodigy Performers understand this and wouldn't want it any other way.

Embracing oneself as the ultimate decision-maker is a powerful acknowledgment of personal agency and responsibility. It underscores the importance of trust in one's intuition, values, and judgment. Life presents an array of choices, from mundane daily decisions to pivotal life-changing moments, and having the self-assurance to make these decisions independently is a testament to one's autonomy. It does not negate seeking advice or considering external input, but it emphasizes the importance of having the final say rooted in one's convictions. This mindset fosters a strong sense of self and encourages accountability, as individuals recognize that their choices shape their paths and outcomes. The empowerment derived from being your own decision-maker also instills resilience, as one learns to stand by their choices, learn from missteps, and celebrate successes with a sense of ownership. It is a journey of cultivating trust in oneself, embracing the role of a decision-maker, and navigating life's complexities with confidence and authenticity.

People, including close friends and family, may not understand or be ready for your journey. It's essential to accept this fact. There's no need to fight it. This doesn't mean you should alter your plans or dilute your hopes and dreams. On the contrary, it likely means you're on the right path to pioneering something new, and you will need to focus on your vision more than ever. Even if it's a few years before you may ultimately have the power to make these decisions for yourself, having everything together and being clear on your focus will allow others to easily support you.

Regrettably, it may also mean that you'll have to leave some people behind. People grow and evolve at different rates. If they matter, they'll catch up when the time is right. Don't let others dictate your growth pace. Sometimes, you need to remove the obstacles so your growth can flourish. On the other side of this challenging transition often lies the opportunity to form healthier relationships and to connect with people who genuinely have your best interests at heart. While navigating this change can be challenging, it ultimately paves the way for more positive and nurturing connections and underscores the importance of quality over quantity in friendships. Embracing this change opens doors to establishing a network that is supportive, understanding, and aligned with one's values, contributing significantly to personal growth and happiness. The decision is yours.

YOUR ONLY TRUE COMPETITION IS YOURSELF

Competition is a construct of your mind; your only true competition is yourself. The ultimate goal is self-improvement and a sense of accomplishment. Competition with others is merely a motivational tool; it isn't real and has no intrinsic value. A win is a win if it propels you closer to your goals and keeps you motivated. A loss is a win if it pushes you toward your desires and maintains your motivation. The labels you attach to these outcomes, like first place or last place, mean very little. They offer a fleeting confidence boost and validate that moment in time. Enjoy the competition, but don't become consumed by counting your victories and losses when measuring your self-worth. It's all a game; learn to play while maintaining your love for it.

Outwork everyone with integrity and keep the ultimate destination in mind. If you bring your career and life goals into the picture, there is no real competition but yourself. There's really no one to "beat," no actual first place or platinum. With this understanding, you can more easily shake off feelings of defeat. By acknowledging that the journey of improvement is ongoing and personal, individuals empower themselves to be proactive in their pursuit of excellence, maintaining motivation from within. In essence, viewing oneself as one's own true competition is about embracing a journey of continuous learning and striving, where the pursuit of personal excellence is the ultimate and most rewarding challenge.

IT'S OKAY TO CHANGE YOUR MIND

It's absolutely okay to change your mind. How will you know unless you try? When you're in tune with your ultimate decision-making power, you can be comfortable changing your mind as often as you like. Prodigy Performers don't make these decisions lightly; each move is carefully planned to better achieve their goals. Don't focus on where you are, but rather on where you're going, and make adjustments accordingly.

Discipline equals freedom. Want more free time? Embrace disciplined time management. Seeking financial freedom? Implement long-term financial discipline. Aspiring to be healthy? Commit to a healthy diet and exercise regimen. Simplifying everything down to an "if-then" format, discipline provides the foundation for freedom.

Be in a hurry to learn, not in a hurry to receive validation. In this age of social media, instant likes can distort this process and make it difficult to follow your own path and make up your mind for yourself. Prodigy Performers understand that likes will come once they've mastered their craft and gained knowledge. Conventional, expected content will always earn easy, meaningless likes. However, unique, groundbreaking content might take time. Many great artists and masters were ahead of their time and often weren't appreciated during their lives. It takes a special person to persist in their pursuit despite this. When you're ultimately reaching your goals and experiencing continued success, you might be surprised by what success means to you. What you thought would bring joy may not deliver as expected, while other aspects will shine. This is natural; the meaning of success and what you value evolves over time. The same Performance habits still apply as you continue on your journey.

ATTRACTING LIKE ENERGIES

"I can't relate to lazy people. We don't speak the same language. I don't understand you. I don't want to understand you." – Kobe Bryant.

You can't please everyone, and you shouldn't even try. Focus on pleasing yourself and surrounding yourself with like-minded individuals. I'm a firm believer that the energy you put out is what comes back to you. Granted that the energy we put out doesn't always come back to us directly or immediately, the general atmosphere and relationships we cultivate through our actions play a significant role in shaping our experiences and opportunities. In essence, being mindful of the energy we radiate encourages a life lived with intention, kindness, and positivity, fostering a cycle of goodwill that benefits both ourselves and the projects we are a part of. Remember, like energies, they gravitate toward each other.

Success brings new, positive energy, so embrace it. Create fresh challenges for yourself regularly, and then work on solving them, and they will continue to appear. It's vital to seize opportunities as they come, not just when they are convenient or obvious. The timing of these opportunities is often beyond your control, but you can position yourself in situations where they are more likely to arise. Your job is to be prepared and to recognize the potential benefits. Sometimes, this can be difficult; if the benefits were clear, the opportunity would have already been seized. Determine what will have the most significant impact, prioritize, and take action.

This may take time. Ideally, everything you desire would happen instantly, but life doesn't always work that way. You're in this for the long game. If you stay the course, you'll find a way. Stay true to your purpose and reinforce the right habits to support it. There may be bumps on the road, but that's when it's time to double down and push harder. Stay focused on your goals, as constantly adding options and making pit stops only lengthens the journey. Choose wisely, but beware of waiting for the perfect moment – that never comes. Get in the game and make sure you're doing all you can right now!

SECTION 10: TIME TO WORK...
WHERE TO START?

"The future depends on what you do today." - Mahatma Gandhi.

If you're wondering what your next steps should be, well, let's get to work! I'm here to guide you through specific actions and suggestions to kickstart each of the 8 Performance Habits. The crucial thing is to start now. Once you set this book aside, days turn into weeks, weeks turn into months, and before you know it, you'll be lamenting, "I should have... I wish I would have... if only I had..." So, make yourself your number one priority and start now. Strive for more, do more, be more!

Get a notebook or device for note-taking and a calendar

CULTIVATING THE RIGHT MINDSET

At this point in the book, you should be well-acquainted with the idea that a proper mindset is crucial for success. It's not only the most important step but also the easiest to master if you put your mind to it. You must firmly believe that anything is possible because you are in complete control of your thoughts and actions. Your reactions to negativity should be rooted in love and positivity, and you must be adept at moving on without dwelling on negative things or people. As a Prodigy Performer, you won't let anything or anyone stand in the way of your ambitions. You've placed yourself on the highest shelf and held yourself accountable. You believe that everything is possible, and it's up to you to determine how hard you work and in which direction.

Action:

• Write your name prominently at the top, followed by "Professional Dancer."

• Write down why you want to be a dancer and what qualities make you perfect for this career. This mission statement is for your eyes only, so be bold and inspiring. It should bring a smile to your face every time you read it.

• Jot down things and people you are thankful for. This cultivates a positive outlook on life, enhancing overall well-being, and reminds you who is on your team and deserving of your energy and attention.

Positive Self-Talk

• Start practicing positive self-talk (This can be in your head and out loud). Regularly affirm your worth and capabilities. Challenge and change negative thoughts about yourself to positive ones.

• Decide on your motivation mantra and develop words or phrases you can think of and say to remind you why you do all of this.

SETTING GOALS AND PLANNING

Now, it's time to plan. While some might advise writing just three goals, I believe in writing down all your goals. You may need a substantial notebook because there's a lot to unpack. You should continually update this list with daily upkeep initially and at least weekly once you get into the habit. Your book is going to be quite comprehensive, but when you can see your path and have a clear plan, it's much easier to follow.

Action:

• Start with your biggest goals and write them down.

Write as many goals as you can think of and keep adding to your list.

• Organize these goals into smaller "sub-goals" that break down your big goals into actionable items.

• Create a timeline for your goals, define clear and achievable objectives, scheduling when you'll achieve them.

• For each goal, define the "who," "how," and "what" that will contribute to your success.

MAINTAINING CLEAR FOCUS AND PERSISTENCE

Now that you have a mission, specific goals, and a plan, you need a clear focus to reach them. You must also have the persistence to see them through. Your goals should now be a priority, and you should never give up. In the beginning, you may need to remind yourself often by referring to your calendar, but this constant reinforcement will keep your focus on what will make you successful.

Action:

• Create a list of skills that will help you succeed in reaching your goals.

• Define how you'll develop these skills through research, practice, or training.

• Determine how much daily time you will devote to remembering and maintaining clear focus. When and what will this look like?

• Every morning, go over your most important goals for the day and remind yourself what you're doing to stay focused and persistent. Revisit these goals throughout your day.

EFFICIENT TRAINING, HEALTHY EATING, AND PROPER SLEEP HABITS

Establish and review your training regimen, both dance and health/exercise-wise. This might require some research and conversations with teachers and coaches. Make sure your training goals are included in your planner and calendar, and keep them updated.

Action:

• List all your classes and workouts and match them to your goals to ensure you're training efficiently and correctly.

• Begin a food journal to track your dietary habits for a week and research what is optimal for your desired body type and goals.

• Start tracking your sleep schedule, ensuring it allows for optimum performance.

Remember, these three habits are vital components of your plan to achieve your goals. Excelling in one or two isn't sufficient. Your body is your instrument, and training for your specific weaknesses is crucial. If you need guidance in any of these aspects, consider enlisting a physical trainer, life coach, or dietitian; it can be one of the best investments in your future.

PRACTICE AND DEDICATION TO YOUR CRAFT

Dedication to your craft is a culmination of the first four habits. A proper mindset, well-defined goals, a detailed plan, unwavering focus, and persistence will all inspire the dedication you need to reach your highest potential. Dedication is more than just training; it encompasses the love for everything about dancing. This includes choreography, improvisation, dance history, and keeping up with current performances. Immerse yourself in the world of dance, research, and practice living the life. Continuous learning and education are invaluable for long-term success.

Action:

• Write down aspects related to dance, such as choreography, improvisation, dance history, and current performances.

• Schedule these activities in your calendar as part of your dedication to your craft.

• Continuously seek learning and education to propel your long-term success.

• If you're without agency representation, establish a plan to seek one. Contact agencies, schedule appointments, and submit your portfolio.

Remember, your journey towards becoming a Prodigy Performer involves mastering all eight Performance Habits, not just one or two. Make a commitment to excellence in every aspect of your dance career.

POLISHING YOUR SOCIAL MEDIA SKILLS AND PRESENTATION

Effectively marketing yourself and presenting a compelling product is crucial. Strong social skills are invaluable in this process, especially in the world of dance. The visual aspect, both on and off the stage, plays a pivotal role in how you're perceived. In today's digital age, social media has become a critical platform for self-presentation. Your profiles act as the face of your business. First impressions matter, and this is a significant advantage of living in today's world. Use it wisely to create an appealing personal brand.

Action:

• Audit all your social media platforms, removing any content that doesn't present you in a positive light.

• Craft a clean and aesthetically pleasing profile that showcases your best qualities.

• Schedule regular posts, maintaining a consistent online presence.

• Your communication and presentation play a substantial role in making an impression. Add these tasks to your calendar and be proactive in following up.

EFFECTIVELY DEALING WITH FAILURE AND SETBACKS

As I've mentioned before, setbacks and failures are a part of life. Managing them effectively is a skill closely tied to the first Performance Habit: mindset. Your mindset determines what you learn from failures. Understanding that failure is a temporary situation and being resilient enough to bounce back makes you unstoppable. Acknowledge your mistakes, extract the lessons, and move forward without letting them define you. A mistake is a signal that your calculations need adjustment, so recalibrate and focus on what did work. Through the development of these habits, you'll make fewer mistakes. Failures will become rare, and setbacks will be minimal as you anticipate and adapt to challenges. True failure only occurs when you run out of options and accept defeat.

Action:

• Collect inspirational quotes about risk, failure, and setbacks in a list.

• Include these quotes in your dance journal and calendar for regular motivation.

• Refer to this list frequently, especially during challenging times, to boost your confidence and resilience.

• Analyze failures objectively and decide what to adjust or whether to cut your losses, take the lesson, and move on.

CONFIDENT LEADERSHIP ABILITIES

Lead by example and invest time and effort in elevating others. Leadership abilities are integral because Prodigy Performers must operate at the highest level without leaving anything to chance. Effective leadership sets high expectations for success and inspires all involved. A leader's confidence in facing whatever challenges arise resonates with everyone, and Prodigy Performers need to thrive in such situations. Once you're recognized as a leader, opportunities will come your way, but until then, don't hesitate to ask for them. Don't be shy; seek out challenges, work, and thrive in your accomplishments.

Action:

• Identify scenarios where you can take on leadership roles and make a list.

• Define the steps you can take to place yourself in these positions.

• Consider creating your own projects.

• Take the initiative in project management on current endeavors and involve others.

As you develop your knowledge, skills, and abilities, these habits will become ingrained. This transformation will lead to confidence and help you become the person you aspire to be. The difficulty of this process is entirely up to you; you decide what's hard or easy in your life. Choose wisely, as Prodigy Performance habits will truly transform your life for the better.

SECTION 11: LET IT FLOW... BE CREATIVE

"I live a creative life. When you put creativity into everything, everything becomes available to you." – Robert Rodriguez.

Once you develop and have consistently established Prodigy Performance habits, it's time to let it flow. You've spent so much time and effort on the structure of things now it's time to "Just Dance." One of the frustrating things I see from many extremely talented people is the lack of just going with it and trusting things to work out. Once your base is set, trust it! Because you have great Prodigy habits, you don't always need to know what you are doing. You trust that your creativity and training will allow you to thrive. There will be many adjustments along the way. The first step is just to begin.

LET IT FLOW

The phrase "let it flow" encapsulates the idea of releasing control, allowing ideas and emotions to move freely, and being open to the natural progression of things. This approach is much needed after a very structured focus on building a great base of Performance Habits. Being able to relax and enjoy your hard work. This practice encourages:

• **Embracing Imperfections:** Understand that not everything needs to be perfect. Sometimes, beauty and innovation come from the unexpected and unplanned.

• **Mindfulness:** Be present in the moment and fully engage with your current task or thought process, letting go of distractions and pressures.

• **Openness to New Experiences:** Be willing to step out of your comfort zone and try new things, as this can lead to unexpected sources of inspiration.

• **Trusting the Process:** Have faith in your abilities and believe that even if things don't make sense now, they will eventually come together.

• **Letting Go of Fear:** Release the fear of judgment or failure, as these fears can hinder your creative flow and prevent you from taking risks.

Looking at someone and saying, "That's great, show me exactly how to do that," or thinking a book like this will give you everything you need is not the answer. You must now get it done in your own way and add your twist to it. Duplicating someone else's talent and process is nearly impossible. Use everything for inspiration and then make it your own. The willingness to be present, jump in with both feet, get started, and then improvise through all the twists and turns is vital. When you get the feeling, "I don't know if I'm doing it right," it's ok; nobody knows. It's always right when it works out, and we change our approach when it does not. Just get the ball rolling and keep moving.

"Learn the rules like a pro, so you can break them like an artist" – Pablo Picasso.

Be Creative:

Creativity is not just about art; it's a way of thinking that encourages innovation and seeing the world from different perspectives. A few ideas to foster creativity:

• **Cultivate Curiosity:** Ask questions and seek to understand the world around you. Curiosity drives exploration and innovative thinking.

• **Make Connections:** Try to connect seemingly unrelated ideas or concepts. This can lead to unique solutions and new ways of thinking.

- **Take Breaks:** Give your brain time to rest and rejuvenate, as this can enhance problem-solving abilities and creative thinking.

- **Create a Supportive Environment:** Surround yourself with other creative individuals and seek environments that stimulate your creativity.

- **Practice Regularly:** Like any skill, creativity improves with practice. Engage in activities that challenge your creative thinking regularly.

- **Embrace Challenges:** View challenges as opportunities to think creatively and develop new solutions.

WORK OUTSIDE THE BOX

Embracing a mentality that encourages thinking and working outside the box can yield numerous benefits, fostering innovation, creativity, and adaptability in dance and life. When you allow yourself to step beyond conventional boundaries and challenge the status quo, you open up a realm of possibilities that can lead to groundbreaking ideas. Workshop anything and everything. Dabble in all sorts of fresh, fun ideas. Choreograph, film, write shows, develop social media projects, there are no limits. This approach encourages a problem-solving mindset that is not confined by pre-established norms or limitations, promoting a culture of continuous learning, experimentation, and improvement. Many times, the thing you thought you were working on morphs into an entirely new and exciting project. This is where the magic happens. The habits and structure you are developing will keep that magic flowing.

Moreover, thinking outside the box enhances your ability to adapt to change, a crucial skill in today's ever-evolving world. It fosters a proactive attitude toward facing challenges, turning potential obstacles into opportunities for growth and development. Not just in you personally but within your ideas and projects.

In essence, thinking and working outside the box is not just about being different for the sake of it; it's about fostering a mindset that values curiosity, embraces challenges, and is continually seeking better and more innovative opportunities. It is a mindset that does not shy away from risks and is open to exploring uncharted territories, ultimately leading to personal and professional growth, innovation, and success. It is the mindset of a Prodigy Performer.

COLLABORATE WITH EVERYONE

Find your tribe. Work with your friends on a collaborative level. Be the catalyst. Providing the opportunity and encouraging diverse and unconventional thinking within teams can lead to a rich pool of ideas, driving innovation and excellence. It promotes an inclusive environment where all voices are valued, and creativity flows with you directing it. This will inspire you and take you in directions others see, but you may not have thought of. Collaboration fosters trust and builds strong relationships among team members. These strengthened relationships can lead to the development of a great support team. Working together allows for cross-checking and validation of ideas. Collaborative environments also foster accountability, ensuring that all aspects of a project are thoroughly reviewed and assessed. Some ideas are great in theory but don't actually work out in reality. Try them anyway! This is why many minds in the game can lead to successful outcomes. It's about that flow and how you can direct it positively and productively. By letting your thoughts and ideas flow freely and embracing your creative potential, you open yourself up to a world of endless possibilities and opportunities.

It's not just about working together; it's about combining strengths, sharing knowledge, and working towards a common goal. By fostering open communication, building trust, and leveraging the diverse skills of each team member, you can create a collaborative environment that drives success, innovation, and positive outcomes. Collaboration is a powerful tool for achieving goals, sparking innovation, and fostering a positive community. Here are some effective ways to collaborate:

Establish Clear Objectives:

• Ensure that every team member understands the goals of the project. Clear objectives provide direction and help in aligning the team's efforts.

Open Communication:

• Encourage open and honest communication. Create an environment where team members feel comfortable sharing their thoughts, ideas, and feedback.

Utilize Diverse Skill Sets:

• Recognize and utilize the diverse skills and strengths of each team member. Assign tasks based on individual strengths to enhance efficiency and effectiveness.

Foster a Culture of Respect:

• Build a culture of mutual respect where each team member's contribution is valued. This encourages active participation and engagement.

Encourage Innovation:

• Create an environment that fosters creativity and innovation. Encourage team members to think outside the box and explore new ideas.

Build Trust:

• Foster trust within the team. Trust is the foundation of effective collaboration and can be built through reliability, openness, and mutual support.

Practice Active Listening:

• Encourage active listening. Make sure that team members are fully engaged and attentive to each other's ideas and feedback.

Use Collaborative Tools:

• Leverage technology and use collaborative tools such as shared documents, project management software, and communication platforms to enhance collaboration.

Celebrate Successes:

• Celebrate the team's achievements and milestones. Recognizing and celebrating successes builds morale and reinforces the value of collaboration.

Be Flexible:

• Be open to adjusting strategies, roles, and plans as needed. Flexibility is key to adapting to changes and overcoming challenges.

Encourage Accountability:

• Establish clear roles and responsibilities. Encourage accountability to ensure that each team member is contributing to the best of their abilities.

Provide Constructive Feedback:

• Give and encourage constructive feedback. Feedback helps in identifying areas for improvement and in recognizing good performance.

SECTION 12: MAY THE FORCE BE WITH YOU...

"Do or do not. There is no try." - Yoda, Star Wars.

<u>Good Luck</u>

Made in the USA
Las Vegas, NV
15 April 2024

88715692R00115